WHAT LA GENTE ARE SAYING ABOUT **CALLADITA NO MORE**

"*Calladita No More* feels like sitting with a wise amiga who sees you, affirms you, and lovingly challenges you to rise. Hady Méndez opens each chapter with a refrán, grounding us in our culture and reminding us that our ancestral wisdom has always been there to guide us. Her tone is warm and invitational, but don't be mistaken because this is a bold call to reject the silence that's been expected of us for too long. Hady masterfully weaves personal storytelling with collective truths, making this book both a mirror and a map."

—**Ana Flores**
Author, and Founder of #WeAllGrow Latina

"We don't need another manual on how to play the game, we need liberation. And *Calladita No More* delivers exactly that. Hady Méndez isn't just telling her story, she's calling out the systems that have kept so many of us quiet, small, and overworked. As someone who has spent years dissecting the impact of Calladita Culture®, I cheered while reading every page. This book is both a mirror and a path, a sacred tool for those ready to remember who they are. It's time to speak louder, take up more space, and rewrite the narrative. And Hady hands us the mic."

—**Pam Covarrubias**
Leadership Coach for Latinas, Creator of
Calladita Culture®, and Host of Café con Pam

"Hady Méndez is that rare truth teller who manages to be relatable, witty, and brilliantly insightful all at once. Reading *Calladita No More* feels like sitting with your bestie amiga: the moment where you can finally exhale, let your guard down, and just be yourself without judgment or pretense. For any mujer looking to take up space, this is a must-have book and love letter to show up unapologetically, as you are."

—**Ruby Garcia**
Leadership & Visibility Coach,
Founder of Ruby Garcia Coaching

"*Calladita No More* is an urgent invitation for all of us—regardless of background—to show up with courage and commitment. Hady Méndez shares her journey with honesty and insight, weaving together personal experiences and broader lessons that challenge us to break out of our comfort zones. As someone who has spent decades amplifying marginalized voices, I see this book as a vital tool to deepen our understanding and strengthen our resolve to support diverse leadership. A must-read for anyone striving to create inclusive spaces where all voices are heard and honored."

—**Jennifer Brown**
Keynote Speaker and Best-Selling Author,
Inclusion, Beyond Diversity and *How to be an Inclusive Leader*

"Reading *Calladita No More* by Hady Méndez was nothing short of transformative. Hady's story felt like hearing my own, finally spoken aloud with honesty and power. Hady doesn't shy away from the realities of being a Latina in environments where our voices are too often silenced or ignored. Instead, she lays it all out—the doubts, the triumphs, and the moments of quiet strength that build into something unstoppable. Reading her words was like permission to take up space, to own my story, and to see my own greatness reflected back. *Calladita No More* is more than a memoir—it's a rallying cry for every Latina who has ever felt unseen. I walked away from this book feeling not just heard, but ready to make my own mark."

—**Dr. Jasmine Escalera**
Founder and Reinvention Strategist

"Bold, authentic and empowering. Hady's *Calladita No More* is a must-read guidebook for all women of color looking to reclaim their power in the modern workplace."

—**Giovanna González**
Award-Winning Author of *Cultura & Cash*

"*Calladita No More* is for every first-gen Latina who has ever been told to shrink to 'make it.' To those with a fire inside they've had to dim to 'fit in.' Hady's raw storytelling and abundant wisdom in this book is a reminder that our voices are not just valid—they're vital."

—**Odalys Jasmine García Arce**
Host of Hella Latin@ Podcast

"*Calladita No More* is a breath of fresh air; a powerful and honest exploration of growth, identity, and comunidad. As Hady Méndez shares her journey, you feel like you're walking alongside her, learning through her experiences and thoughtful guidance. This book is both a call to awareness and a guide toward empowered action, not by leaving your identity, culture, and values behind, but by harnessing them as a guiding light."

—**Vanessa Schwippert**
Founder of the Latina Writing Comunidad

"I was hooked from the start. In *Calladita No More*, Hady shares her journey to corporate America as a first-gen Latina. Hady shares how she navigated racism, microaggressions, imposter syndrome, a calladita mindset, the lack of representation, and so much more. I felt seen in her experiences and I appreciate her candid and straight up voice. She did not sugar coat or hold back. Thank you for enabling me to feel seen and empowered."

—**Alyssa Reynoso-Morris**
Children's Book Author, Speaker, Mentor and Mother

"Hady shows us that sometimes the greatest acts of leadership are the ones we practice with ourselves: choosing faith over fear, perspective over panic, and purpose over ego. Her book will serve as a masterclass in grace, grit, and staying ready for what's next."

—**Minda Harts**
Author of The Memo

"Every Latina will see herself in these pages. In Hady's story, and in the strength and resilience of the mujeres she uplifts, I see myself—and I know so many Latinas will too. *Calladita No More* is the guide we've been waiting for: it gives us the permission, language, and confidence to break free from the cultural and societal pressures that have kept us small or silent. Latinas have always been leaders, but now we have a roadmap that helps us claim our power, unapologetically, for ourselves and for the next generation. Bold, honest, and fiercely empowering—this is essential reading for any Latina ready to pave her own path and amplify her voice."

—**Ashley K. Stoyanov Ojeda**
Author of *Jefa in Training*

CALLADITA NO MORE

CALLADITA NO MORE

My Latina Journey and the
Lessons that Shaped Me

HADY MÉNDEZ

Copyright © 2025 Hady Méndez. All rights reserved.

No part of this publication shall be reproduced, transmitted, or sold in whole or in part in any form without prior written consent of the author, except as provided by the United States of America copyright law. Any unauthorized usage of the text without express written permission of the publisher is a violation of the author's copyright and is illegal and punishable by law. All trademarks and registered trademarks appearing in this guide are the property of their respective owners.

For permission requests, write to the publisher, addressed "Attention: Permissions Coordinator," at the address below.

Publish Your Purpose
141 Weston Street, #155
Hartford, CT 06141

The opinions expressed by the Author are not necessarily those held by Publish Your Purpose.

Ordering Information: Quantity sales and special discounts are available on quantity purchases by corporations, associations, and others. For details, contact the author at hola@calladitanomore.com.

Edited by: Sandra Wissinger, Johanie Martinez-Cools
Cover illustration by: Sol Cotti
Cover design: Nelly Murariu
Typeset by: Medlar Publishing Solutions Pvt Ltd., India

ISBN: 979-8-88797-175-9 (hardcover)
ISBN: 979-8-88797-176-6 (paperback)
ISBN:979-8-88797-177-3 (ebook)

Library of Congress Control Number: 2025910529

First edition, September 2025.

The information contained within this book is strictly for informational purposes. The material may include information, products, or services by third parties. As such, the Author and Publisher do not assume responsibility or liability for any third-party material or opinions. The publisher is not responsible for websites (or their content) that are not owned by the publisher. Readers are advised to do their own due diligence when it comes to making decisions.

Publish Your Purpose is a hybrid publisher of non-fiction books. Our mission is to elevate the voices often excluded from traditional publishing. We intentionally seek out authors and storytellers with diverse backgrounds, life experiences, and unique perspectives to publish books that will make an impact in the world. Do you have a book idea you would like us to consider publishing? Please visit PublishYourPurpose.com for more information.

"El sacrificio de hoy, es el éxito de mañana."[1]

This book is dedicated to my late mother, Aida Esther Méndez Cruz.

Mami was una mujer humilde who was born in Aguadilla, Puerto Rico; got married in her mid-twenties; had two daughters; moved to Brooklyn, NY; had two more daughters; and dedicated herself to her familia.

Mami never went to college, never held a corporate job, never had a bank account or a credit card, yet she taught her four daughters how to be strong, powerful women.

I will never forget how she instilled in me the desire to want more, be more, and expect more out of life.

I learned to be brave and bold because of my mother.

---

[1] This refrán loosely translates to "The sacrifice of today leads to the success of tomorrow." This refrán emphasizes the notion that success is not something that happens overnight. We must work hard and make sacrifices today that will lead to our future successes. Persistence is the key message of this refrán.

Every woman
who refuses to be silent
helps another woman
find her voice.

—Simone de Beauvoir

TABLE OF CONTENTS

FOREWORD — xvii

PRIMERO QUE NADA — xxiii

CHAPTER 1
THE ROLE OF FAMILIA — 1

CHAPTER 2
CONFÍA IN YOU — 15

CHAPTER 3
SAVE THE DRAMA FOR YOUR MAMA — 25

CHAPTER 4
DESCUBRIENDO YOUR WHY — 39

CHAPTER 5
FIRST, BUILD COMUNIDAD   51

CHAPTER 6
SELF-CARE, SIEMPRE   65

CHAPTER 7
MUJER, TAKE UP SPACE   79

CHAPTER 8
NADIE IS COMING TO SAVE YOU   93

CHAPTER 9
BE YOU SIN EXCUSAS   105

CHAPTER 10
STEADFAST Y POSITIVA   119

CHAPTER 11
BRING OTHERS CONTIGO   131

CHAPTER 12
AHORA, IT'S YOUR TURN   143

ACKNOWLEDGEMENTS   155

ABOUT THE AUTHOR   161

FOREWORD

In a world that so often tries to quiet us, Hady Méndez rises, bold, unapologetic, and unwavering. She reminds us that our voices matter, our stories carry strength, and our identities are not just worth celebrating—they are a source of power. By embracing her truth, she not only shapes her own future but lifts others along the way, clearing a path for those still searching for theirs. Her journey is a powerful reminder that when we lead with authenticity and courage, we don't just transform our own lives, we create space for others to rise too.

As the founder and president of Lean In Latinas, I've dedicated my career to empowering Latinas to rise to their fullest potential: personally, professionally, and unapologetically. I've witnessed the strength, brilliance, and unwavering resilience Latinas bring to the workplace, and I'm honored to stand alongside those who are boldly forging paths in industries where we've long been underrepresented. Hady Méndez is one of those trailblazers. Through her work, she embodies what it means to lead with purpose, serving not only as a role model, but as a powerful force of strength, courage, and inspiration. She has created space and given voice to countless Latinas, empowering them to share their talents, own their stories, and take their place in the rooms where they rightfully deserve to be.

I first met Hady only briefly, but even in that short moment, her passion and unwavering commitment to elevating underrepresented voices were undeniable. In the two years since, I've had the true privilege of working alongside her, witnessing not only her professional brilliance but also the personal growth we've both experienced on this journey. What continues to move me most about Hady is her authenticity. She shows up fully, not just as a leader, but as a deeply compassionate and intentional human being who is genuinely invested in the success and well-being of those around her. She believes in pouring into others, lifting them up, and celebrating their victories as if they were her own. She's the kind of mujer (woman) who claps—loudly and often—for others, never hesitating to acknowledge and cheer for the accomplishments of those she believes in. What began as a simple introduction has grown into a meaningful partnership grounded in shared purpose and values. I've seen firsthand how she uses her voice and her platform to empower others to take bold, unapologetic steps forward in their lives and careers and she does it all with heart, humility, and fierce dedication.

Hady is uniquely positioned to write this book. Her own journey is a powerful testament to everything she teaches others: take ownership of your story, lead with intention, and fight for your place in spaces where you've often been overlooked. With more than three decades of experience in both corporate and leadership roles, Hady has made it her mission to empower underrepresented communities—especially Latinas and Women of Color—to thrive in their careers. She's not just a thought leader; she's lived through the challenges and celebrated the triumphs of breaking barriers in the workplace, making her wisdom and insights all the more impactful.

Foreword

Get ready to be fired up! This book isn't just another career guide. It's a game-changer for anyone who's ever felt overlooked, underestimated, or silenced in their professional journey. Hady's insights come straight from her own powerful experiences and offer a no-nonsense roadmap to reclaim your power, demand your worth, and own your leadership with unstoppable confidence. Hady doesn't just talk the talk, she's walked the walk, and now she's showing you exactly how to break through. This book will completely shift the way you see leadership and make you realize just how much potential you have to step into your own power and purpose.

Anna Dapelo-Garcia, MPA-HSA
Founder & President, Lean In Latinas
April 2025

PRIMERO QUE NADA

"Si no sabes de dónde vienes,
no sabrás adónde vas."[2]

---

[2]This refrán loosely translates to "If you don't know where you come from, you'll never know where you're going." This refrán is highlighting the importance of understanding your roots, cultural background, and personal history. All of these are essential to making informed decisions that shape your future. Self-awareness is the key message of this refrán.

I remember the day like it was yesterday. But the year was more like 1993. It was a Saturday morning, and I was at my client site because I was a consultant and that's what you do on a Saturday morning when you have that kind of job. I was dressed down because we were allowed to come in casual on the weekends. My colleagues waited for me in the lobby so we could go up together. "You grab the keys," they said. "We'll wait over here." So, off I went to ask the security guard for the keys to the test lab, where we'd spend the next eight hours running scripts to assess the viability of our client's software.

What happened next was something I never could have expected. Imagine how traumatizing it was that thirty years later, I can still remember not only the incident but how it made me feel.

ME: "Hey there, I'm here for the keys to the test lab on the second floor."

SECURITY GUARD: "Are you here to clean it?"

ME: *Shock. Silence. Humiliation.*

ME (eventually): "No, I'm not here to clean it. I'm a consultant and I'm here to do my job. I need the keys to the second-floor test lab."

I'd like to say that this story is made up. That it never happened to me. Or that I never experienced another microaggression at work. But you and I know that as Latinas, shit like this happens all the time. People sometimes mistake us for the cleaning lady or the secretary because, let's be real, that's where they think we belong.

I want to be abundantly clear: being a cleaning lady or a secretary is honorable, necessary work. The issue I have is the assumption that, as Latinas, we couldn't possibly hold roles with more power, influence, or visibility.

So how do we challenge these stereotypes and show up differently? Are we taking up space and using our voice to demand the respect we rightfully deserve? Are we able to quickly respond and shut down microaggressions or do incidents like the one I shared keep us silent and small? There's a lot I have to say on this topic, but I don't want to get ahead of myself so let's start from the beginning.

Hija de Brooklyn and Puerto Rico

Born in Brooklyn to Puerto Rican parents, I'm proud to call myself a Nuyorican. I am the youngest of four sisters. We grew up in the projects in an area of Brooklyn that was predominantly Black and Brown. My mom and dad never went to college, but my sisters and I all did. I was the first to live in a dorm in my whole family! I graduated from college with a 3.98 GPA. This allowed me to secure a job at a great consulting company. I had the goal of earning $100K by the time I was thirty and I achieved that goal. I love technology and working with customers and have gone on to have a long career at the intersection of technology and financial services.

Being Latina showed up for me in a lot of ways: I didn't get promoted at the same rate as my peers, I wasn't earning the same as my non-Latinx counterparts, and I was often overlooked and underestimated at work. I felt just as qualified as my peers, and was getting comparable outcomes in my work, but I still felt like people didn't see my contributions or simply chose to ignore them. It was hard not having a mentor or coach to help me navigate company politics or make me see that I needed to show up differently. I felt very unwelcome and excluded even when I was invited to meetings. And I think you might relate to this: When you don't feel welcome, it's hard to do your best work. I was constantly second-guessing myself and almost never contributed to the conversation for fear that I would say something wrong or stupid. I felt like an imposter in many of these spaces, and I did not want to be found out.

When I look back, there was a lot at play here. My upbringing, limiting beliefs, a lack of representation, a broken system, and so much more. What I have learned since is that despite all the things working against me, I could still create a situation where I could thrive. I'm not gonna lie and say it was easy, because it wasn't. Shit, I'm still in the fight. But what I will say is that it's possible. And I'm going to share with you what worked for me.

Why we struggle

I don't know about you, but I learned some pretty messed up things from my family and culture. Things like "Because I said so," "Don't talk back to authority figures," or "If you don't have something nice to say, don't say anything at all." When I look back at these lessons,

I discovered they didn't serve me. Even more than that, they were holding me back.

Then I think about the lack of representation, or role models, we experience. We don't usually have people who look like us that are "doing it right." That means, we often try to use non-Latinx men or women as our role models, and that doesn't always work because it doesn't feel natural or authentic.

At the end of the day, the system is broken and that's a big reason why it's not working for us. It wasn't designed for us or with us in mind. That often means we must work twice as hard to prove our worth, and even then, we are paid almost half of what our white male peers earn for the same job. THE SAME JOB. How wild is that?

We don't have to remain powerless

I found a way to reclaim my power. By that, I mean I found a way to use my voice, take up space, and uplift others. To me, these are the core tenets of owning your narrative and walking in your power.

I believe we all have what it takes to change our reality. This includes you.

"But, Hady, you don't understand the politics where I work or the manager I report to." You're right, I don't. What I do know is that we all have the power within us to choose every aspect of our journey. That means we can reject what doesn't serve us and do more of what works.

Not everyone will want to see us be bold and brave as we step into our power. Some will try to hold us back or tell us that what we want or hope for is out of reach. "Know your place" or "Stay in your lane." All code for "Don't rock the boat because who knows what might happen if you do."

I'm here to say amazing things can happen if you choose to say YES to yourself.

You can command any room with confidence and strength.

You can trust yourself so deeply that second-guessing becomes a thing of the past.

You can spot "your people" anywhere because the values and the purpose that connect you is undeniable.

You can remain positive and steadfast in the face of adversity, trusting that the Universe is aligned with you and that what's meant for you will never pass you by.

You can be 100 percent unapologetically you, and while everybody might not like it, they sure as hell will respect it.

Are you ready for this transformation? Let's get started!

What worked for me

Over the course of my over thirty-year career, I learned and experienced so much. I want to share it all with you because I am the person I am today because of all of it.

I'm a corporate veteran. Over two decades at the intersection of technology and financial services gave me a front-row seat to just about every scenario you can imagine.

I'm a sought-after public speaker and a staunch advocate for underestimated talent. I'm an inclusion and belonging evangelist, a writer of articles and essays, and a LinkedIn content creator.

When I'm not speaking, writing, or advocating, you can find me leading a feel-good book club at the local independent bookstore where I work.

I'm bold and audacious. I'm not afraid to share my ideas, opinions, or objections. No matter where I am or what situation I find myself in. I believe what I have to say is valuable and I'm not afraid to take up space. If something I want doesn't exist, I'll be the one to create it. I believe in progress over perfection and will get shit done. I'm the person everyone *should* want on their team.

I'm aware that some people are not comfortable around people like me: an outspoken Woman of Color who isn't focused on optics or politics but committed to telling the truth, empowering others, and challenging the status quo. Some people would prefer that I remain silent or in the background. But that's just not how I roll.

In this book, I'm going to tease out the lessons that I feel were most important on my journey to the Latina I've become. When I think about the key areas that really allowed me to step into my power and show up unapologetically, three things come up for me:

1. **Taking up space:** Yes, I'm talking about physical space, but I am also talking about taking risks, going above and beyond, and making it known that you are in the room or at the table. It's about disrupting the status quo and forcing others to slow down to hear your opinion, consider your recommendation, or acknowledge your objection.
2. **Using my voice:** This is exactly what it sounds like. It's speaking up when you agree, disagree, have questions, are curious, have concerns, or want to raise a red flag. It's advocating for yourself when you're looking to get promoted or a raise. It's sharing the accomplishments you're proud of without fear, shame, or judgement. It's speaking out against a microaggression or biased statement. It's all these things and more.

3. **Showing up for others:** You're going to notice something about me that's not unique but isn't how everyone uses their power and influence. I like to help others shine. I want to see other people succeed. I know there's enough for all of us and so I will always take up space and use my voice not only on behalf of myself, but also on behalf of others. Others could be other women, other Latinx, other underrepresented people, other underestimated people, etc. I will always use my voice to show up for others, especially folks who might not have a seat at the table or a voice in the room. That's the responsibility of an inclusive leader and I very much identify this way.

As you read the chapters ahead, I want you to be open to the messages I share. The order the lessons appear in is intentional. There are some foundational skills you will need to build on your journey. They set the groundwork for what comes next. I also acknowledge that our growth and transformation aren't linear. Sometimes we learn a skill and then enter an environment that forces us to relearn the lesson. That's OK. None of us are perfect so our journeys won't be either. There will be ebbs and flows and that's to be expected. Yet over time, the stuff sticks. We learn to navigate new challenges by digging into our toolbox. We start to recognize patterns, behaviors, and situations, and can trust ourselves to navigate those experiences because we've navigated them before.

What's next

Believe me when I tell you that you have everything you need to begin or continue your journey to be "calladita no more." You hold the same power as me. I hope this book helps you unleash it in a way that serves you, your family, and your community. As a reminder, I will share what worked for me. Take what you want, leave the rest. This is not a blueprint to "Latina success," but it is a real-life example of what someone who shares your identity did to change the trajectory of her life and career.

Use this book to inform whatever changes you want to make to reclaim your power. Take notes, highlight phrases or sections that really resonate with you, journal your responses to reflection questions, and otherwise use the insights you gain to create a personal plan for how you will show up for yourself and others. This is your journey and yours alone. Create the life you want for yourself. I'll be here to cheer you on!

CHAPTER 1

THE ROLE OF FAMILIA

"De tal palo, tal astilla."[3]

---

[3] This refrán loosely translates to "From such a stick, such a splinter." But that makes no sense. So, think of it more akin to "Like mother, like daughter." This refrán is highlighting that children often inherit traits, behaviors, or characteristics from their parents. Said differently, the way someone is raised has a lot to do with how they show up. Family legacy is the key message of this refrán.

My mother was a badass, but I didn't always see her that way. She raised four daughters who all graduated from college, some of us even got advanced degrees and credentials. She didn't have a degree or profession of her own but that didn't stop her from making us all feel that we could achieve great things.

She grew up in a different time. A time when you got married, raised your children, had dinner ready for your husband when he got home, etc. Yet, when I look back on the things she said and did, I feel like she was low-key teaching us how to be bold and brave. It was a "do as I say not as I do" type of situation with Mami. Let me share a quick story with you of a time when she really surprised me.

My ex-husband is a big tattoo fan. When I was with him, I got two tattoos. They are in places where most people can't see them so it might come as a surprise to some people reading this book that I even have any.

Anyways, when I got my first tattoo, I didn't mention it to my mother. I didn't think she would approve of me having a tat and I no longer lived in her house, so it was easy to hide.

A few months after I got said tattoo, I wore a top that revealed the tat when I bent over. Sure enough, she saw it. "¿Qué es eso en tu espalda?" she asked. Crap, I was busted. So, I fessed up. "That's just a little tattoo I got in the form of the Puerto Rican coquí." "Let me see it," she said. So, I pulled up my shirt and let her have a good look. "Te gusta, Mami?" I asked. "Sí," she responded. "I always wanted one."

This story reminds me that the messages we get from our families really matter. The tattoo meant a lot to me to start with, but her approval made me love it even more.

Looking back, that small moment unlocked something even bigger for me. It helped me see the beautiful contradiction that was my mother. She was very conservative in the way she moved, yet there was a side to her that was feisty and unafraid to push back against society's expectations.

While my mother couldn't always model the life she wanted for us, she was clear about what was important: education, a profession, financial security, and family.

With time, I've come to see familia as a rich source of learning when we allow ourselves to notice what's just beyond the surface.

Sometimes, the actions and behaviors of our family are the guides we need to set on the right path, teaching us lessons we might not fully understand at the time but that become clear later.

Sometimes, the lessons we learn from them take root so deeply that they shape the way we move through the world for the rest of our lives.

And sometimes, we draw on what we learn from them as we tackle life's challenges, feeling their guidance shape our decisions and actions.

That's how it is with families. The conversations we have, the approvals we receive, the stories we are told, they stay with us. It's inescapable and unavoidable.

Whether we like it or not, the lessons we learn from our families shape us. If we ignore these lessons, we are missing a part of who we are. We are missing the gifts that our parents and grandparents intended for us to have. We are ignoring the gifts from our ancestors. We are "skipping a step" on the journey to becoming who we are meant to be.

Don't skip this step. Take time to reflect on how your family has shown up for you and the invaluable wisdom they've passed down.

One of the best gifts my mom passed down to me is the gift of refránes. You've seen them already and will continue to see them throughout this book because they are precious to me. I knew when I wrote this book that I would share refránes as part of my journey because they have informed how I show up in spaces, the beliefs I hold, and the lens through which I view the world. What we learn from our families can be both invaluable and messy. Some lessons serve their purpose in a moment and are meant to be released, while others stay with us forever. In this chapter I will share lessons I learned from my late sister, father, and mother.

What I learned from my sister

Before I tell you the story about what I learned from my sister Sonia I want to tell you a little about her and our relationship.

She was my second oldest sister. Remember, I'm the baby in the family. Sony, as we called her, was kind, thoughtful, and smart. While growing up, she had scoliosis and had to wear a back brace for many years. You should google what those braces were like in the eighties because they were horrific. I believe that setback played a significant role in shaping her character. Sonia was insightful and mature.

I trusted her because, despite experiencing this hardship early on, she remained incredibly positive and fair.

The conversation I'm going to share with you occurred in the late seventies/early eighties. I'm not sure how old I was but I would guess I was about ten. That would make Sonia about seventeen. There were protests going on in the streets of our Brooklyn neighborhood around police brutality. These days it would be the equivalent of a Black Lives Matter march.

I asked Sonia why the people were mad and taking to the streets and she explained that a Black man was killed or hurt by White police officers. "I see. Will this lead to a war between Blacks and Whites?" I asked. I don't remember her answer but I remember what I asked next. "If there was a war between Black and White people, what side would we be on?"

Before I share what she told me, I have to share that my question made her pause because I'm not sure she knew the answer. I will also share that over forty years later, this question might still make members of our community pause. Yet her answer gave me the clarity I needed in that moment, and I've carried her response with me ever since.

"I think we would be on the Black side," she said. "Because we have a lot of the same struggles."

That one conversation opened my eyes to the importance of speaking out against injustice as well as understanding my role as a person of color within the broader cultural context. I would reflect on what my sister said that day many times in the years that followed. Talk about a teachable moment!

From my sister Sonia I learned to align myself with people who share my lived experience.

As I look back on this lesson, I believe it sparked my deep admiration and respect for Black women. I've come to see them as role models, showing me how to be brave and strong, advocate for myself, and stand up for what's right.

I have so much love and appreciation for the 92 percent. Their example is a constant reminder of what's possible if you're brave enough.

What I learned from Papá

My father had a shoe store for as long as I can remember. It was called El Encanto Shoes: Shoes for the Entire Family. The "Encanto" part of the name was a nod to our Puerto Rican roots. Puerto Rico is known as La Isla del Encanto or The Island of Enchantment.

My sisters and I all worked at my dad's shoe store at one time or another. Sometimes selling shoes, but mostly working the register. He most trusted his family when it came to dealing with money, so I worked as a cashier from a very early age.

Yes, we got paid. It was a job. And we had shifts and everything.

I usually came in Saturday afternoon after going to CCD/religious education class and would stay till closing.

It would get mad busy during the holidays and for graduations. His store was located on Graham Avenue in Brooklyn. Graham Avenue is also known as La Avenida de Puerto Rico. I know, so many connections back to the motherland. I didn't realize it growing up, but it was really special to live in a neighborhood that was for us by us. Our neighborhood had Puerto Rican-owned bakeries, bodegas, restaurants, travel agencies, and more. Looking back, that was pretty dope.

Most of the people that came to my father's shoe store were from the neighborhood. That means they were mostly Puerto Rican but generally Latinx. Many only spoke Spanish which was fine because being bilingual was our superpower. It was pretty cool to have a front-row seat as my father ran his business. And it was nice to play a role in it. People were often shocked when I greeted them at the age of ten or eleven. I climbed the high ladder to grab shoes in their sizes, answered questions about what colors the shoes came in, and then rang them up. As you can imagine, I loved ringing up customers because I could work the register. My father almost never charged his customers tax to gain customer loyalty. And trust me it worked because when they came back, they would always remind me, "Mingo no me cobra tax" or "Mingo doesn't charge me tax."

I remember we would occasionally have immigrants from other countries come to the store. They would bring in thick string or yarn that represented the shoe size of each person in their family. My dad would patiently take each piece and say, "OK, who is this for?" It was mostly for children. And whenever folks bought multiple pairs of shoes, my dad would give them a discount on top of not charging them tax. Our customers were working-class folks and so were we. But my dad's shoe store was not just a place of business. It was a place where community members could stretch their dollars to get shoes for everyone in their family. My dad knew his role in our community and always ran his business this way.

What I learned from my dad in those early years was that a business can be a business or it can be a service to the community. My dad always prided himself in the latter. Everyone knew Mingo and they knew they could come to his store and find a welcoming space, fashionable shoes, and a business owner who saw customers beyond a way to make money.

This lesson remains with me still. And I would say that I 100 percent follow his business philosophy.

What I learned from Mami

My mom was mostly what I would consider old school. She was not super strict as I was growing up, but when she said "NO," I trusted that the answer was no, and she would not be changing her mind.

My mom didn't go to college or work in a professional environment. Nevertheless, I would consider her to be quite sensible. After all, it was my mom who suggested I study "computers," her word for the field. Who knew that one piece of advice would set me on the path to a long and fulfilling career in tech? I mean, come on, she called it back in the 1980s!

Then there were other moments. I remember when I was dating my first husband, and she told me, "O te casas o lo dejas," meaning "Marry him or break up with him." Those were my two choices after dating him for about one year. Yikes!

The story I want to share with you happened when I graduated from college. It was assumed that after spending four years in school, I would go out and get a professional job. So, I took a job as a technology consultant and went on my merry way. This was back in the nineties when you worked eighty-hour weeks, and nobody batted an eye. It was a tough job (great people, though) and I learned a lot during my time there. Even so, I often questioned whether the work was truly aligned with my values and purpose.

I graduated from a Catholic college where I majored in computer information systems and minored in religious studies. I was very involved in campus ministry, led student retreats, even started a group called Christ in Your Life, or CIYL as it came to be known. During one of my spring breaks, I took a trip to Appalachia and did volunteer work along with my fellow students. I had a heart for the intersection of faith and service but didn't know how to lean into that once I started my consulting gig.

As I was exploring my options, I was considering joining the Peace Corp and traveling to another country. I was afraid to tell my mom because (again) she was old school, and I wasn't sure how it would fly with her. One day I got the courage to tell her that I applied or was considering it (I forget which) but she was having none of it. She felt so strongly that she said, "You will travel to another country over my dead body." Woooow. Needless to say, I took her words to heart and decided not to go. That was back in the early nineties when I was still in my twenties.

Fast forward to today, guess who went on a two-year service trip to South America and worked with incarcerated and formerly incarcerated women? That would be me. I'll be talking more about that experience later in the book as it was truly transformational. What I want you to take away now, though, was that I never lost sight of my dreams. And when the right moment came, I went after the thing my heart deeply desired.

I was clear on my values and purpose very early on. But like a good, obedient daughter, I didn't always act on what I knew my heart wanted because it was either frowned upon or just not the right time. Many say timing is everything and I couldn't agree more. When the time was right, I took my trip and had the experience of a lifetime. I was about ten to twenty years older than the other missioners but that was fine. I used my life experiences to give the best of myself to the people I encountered during my time in Bolivia.

What I learned from my mother was to be thoughtful when making big decisions and consider all the impact your decisions might have.

- Is this the best time to make this decision?
- Do I have the financial resources to support this plan?
- How will this decision impact other people?

I think back to when I finally decided to go overseas. I had money in the bank that I used to live my best life, travel, and be generous with my friends. That was just one good reason to hold off on taking the trip. But then I think about how I also worked as a business consultant during my time in Bolivia. A position I could not have held when I was in my twenties.

My mom was mostly a sensible woman. I credit her for teaching me the value of being thoughtful as you walk through the world and always being mindful of the impact your decisions might have on others. I also learned to stay true to my values and to be patient as the right time came for the things I wanted.

I thought her "advice" (i.e., you will go over my dead body) was pretty crappy at the time. But in hindsight, I respect her insights. She was looking out for me and forcing me to be sure about the actions I was going to take. She was preventing me from acting on a whim and doing something I might later regret.

From Mami, I learned to make decisions I could stand behind. Decisions that are intentional, well-thought-out and genuine reflections of what I want out of life.

Today, I walk confidently in my purpose because of that valuable lesson. And for that I am forever grateful.

En resumen

Our early years shape us. For good and bad. Luckily for me, I was able to learn some very valuable lessons early on. I hope you've had the chance to do the same. If your family is like mine, they want the best for you. And everything they do and say is with that intention in mind.

Even so, be aware of what messages you've received through the years and how they affect the things you believe, say, or do. If you think a message you received early on is holding you back from stepping into the person you are meant to be, be brave enough to shed said belief and replace it with a mindset that invites abundance into your life.

The lessons I grew up with mostly helped to build me into a strong, confident woman. And boy am I ever grateful for that confidence and positive self-worth. There was still shit that I needed to work through, but I realize now that I had a good starting point.

I hope my early stories have encouraged you to reflect on your own journey. To help you dig deeper, here are some questions to consider. The invitation to journal still stands; it can be a powerful way to uncover insights and notice things you might have overlooked before.

1. What lessons did you learn at an early age?

   _____
   _____
   _____
   _____

2. How have these lessons shaped your belief system?

   _____

   _____

   _____

3. How do these beliefs influence your choices today?

   _____

   _____

   _____

4. What beliefs no longer align with the person you are becoming?

   _____

   _____

   _____

CHAPTER 2

CONFÍA IN YOU

"Al mal tiempo, buena cara."[4]

---

[4]This refrán loosely translates to "In bad times, put on a good face." This refrán is spotlighting the need to remain steadfast and positive in the face of adversity. You must truly believe in yourself and your abilities during difficult or challenging situations. That is what will get you through the hard times. Resilience and optimism are the key messages of this refrán.

I spent more than twenty-five years in corporate. During that time, many of my roles were customer facing. I would 1000 percent consider myself a "customer advocate," always looking out for the best interests of the people I worked with and finding new ways to delight them or make their experience even better than they hoped for.

I brought my full self to these roles, embracing my identities, unique strengths, and even the traits others might have perceived as weaknesses. For example, I've always been told, "You talk too much." That was the one thing teachers would always comment on when I was a kid. But the truth is I'm extroverted and love connecting with other people. So, I've learned to see that as a personal strength. It's through authentic conversations and genuine curiosity that I've been able to foster collaboration and open doors for deeper working relationships. By owning all parts of who I am, I've been able to show up with confidence and help others feel seen and valued too.

A few years ago, I worked at a company that hosted an annual convening of their executives. This gathering was meant for the most senior leaders and included the CEO, board members, celebrities, and other bigwigs.

One year, I was invited to attend this meeting. I found out just a few weeks before the event and was extremely excited at the opportunity that was being offered to me. Even though I was not a member of senior management, my leadership team thought it would be a good idea for me to be there to represent my part of the organization.

As I was shopping for my "resort casual" clothes, I started to feel nervous. The more outfits the sales associate brought out for me to try on, the more and more worried I became. I got the worst case of imposter syndrome I've ever experienced. I was very worried that people would wonder what I was doing at the off-site. I was concerned that my clothes wouldn't be as nice as the next person because let's face it, "resort casual" is fine but it was not my vibe, and I wasn't sure I could pull it off. I was nervous about conversations I would be having with senior leaders, one more senior than the other. I did not feel confident in my abilities to say the right thing, sound interesting and smart, or justify being invited to attend this event.

As I was deep in my feelings, I shared my thoughts with a few colleagues and friends. Everyone was super encouraging as I expected. There was another Latina who was also invited and who was equally as nervous. We decided to be there for each other throughout the event which essentially meant hyping each other up between sessions, hanging out during breaks, and telling each other about the surprising conversations we were having at our tables. I was extremely grateful to have someone like me to talk to and share with, and I'm happy that we decided to buddy up the way we did. It really helped me to get through the event all while managing to have a little fun.

When I think back to this event, I wonder if the leaders had any idea what a hard time some of us were having. My guess is that they thought it was a great opportunity for us, which it was. But I doubt they knew that some of us felt like fish out of water.

Latina experiences

Like everyone else, I was hoping to take full advantage of the networking opportunities presented by being at this event. All the while making sure I wasn't coming across as too much or not enough.

That's a thing. You probably know what I'm talking about.

Are the hoop earrings too much for this resort casual setting? Is my laugh too loud? Is my Brooklyn accent too thick? Am I talking to this person for too long and are they bored with what I'm talking about? Am I contributing enough to the conversation? Is it OK to say "where I'm from" or would that just make me come across as an outsider? Do I know enough to carry a conversation or am I coming across as uninformed? Should I sit here and smile politely as folks talk about their golf game or most recent ski trip or should I talk about my hobbies and interests? Do I mention that I graduated from a small, local college or is it better to keep that information to myself?

A lot of shit was coming up for me.

I would never say that remaining "calladita" was a comfortable position for me, but I will admit that sometimes not saying anything is easier. So you don't make a mistake or say something that makes you sound uneducated or misguided.

At this event, I had to fight every instinct that told me to stay quiet and remain in the background. Instead, I chose to show up authentically. I'm a natural leader, I'm positive, I love to laugh, and I'm passionate about social justice, podcasts, and street art. If I was going to stay true to myself, I had to bring all that with me. I'm proud to report that little by little I incorporated parts of myself into the conversations I had and with the people I met.

You may be wondering how I got to that point. If I'm honest, it was a combination of things.

- I came up with an answer to the question "What are you doing here?" or more pointedly, "I didn't think I would see you here." It helped me feel prepared and confident. My response went something like "My leadership tapped me to represent my department and I'm so excited to be part of this experience."
- If I wanted other people to believe that I belonged there, I had to convince myself first. So I had a talk with myself. I said, "Self, you belong here just as much as the next person. This opportunity was given to you and you will make the most of it. Your voice matters and your opinion does too. Show up fully."

Showing up with intention made all the difference. I focused on enjoying the moment, the conversations I was having, and the people I was meeting without any added pressure. Staying in the present moment allowed me to feel more grounded and less concerned about what others might think or say.

Confidence is a feeling from deep inside

Confidence signals to us that we're OK in a situation. That we can handle what's coming. That we can draw from our life experiences and knowledge to navigate challenges with grace and resilience. Confidence is not about being perfect but about trusting ourselves and our ability to figure things out, no matter what comes our way. Having confidence does not mean you will always get the outcomes you hope for. But it does mean that you believe in yourself enough to take on difficult conversations or situations and feel like you tried your best.

We all have the ability to be confident. All it takes is courage to summon it to the surface. It can be called upon at any time by committing to being brave, stepping forward, and believing that you are good enough just as you are.

One confidence-building strategy that's worked well for me is staying curious and open to learning. You should be good at your craft, that goes without saying. But it also helps to be informed. That's where my passion for podcasts comes in handy. The podcasts I listen to keep me current and in the know while helping me understand a little bit about a lot of things. Being able to engage in a variety of conversations has helped me to feel less nervous when connecting with new people, especially folks I initially thought I had little in common with.

To feel confident, it's just as important to remain clear on your values, the impact you want to make, and your higher purpose. This inner compass becomes your North Star, helping you navigate any situation with clarity and authenticity.

The choice is yours

When I was in high school, the song "The Choice is Yours" by Black Sheep was very popular. The lyrics proclaimed, "You can get with this or you can get with that." That's exactly how confidence works because it can mean different things to different people:

- Sometimes, confidence looks like speaking out or taking up space.
- Other times, it's about listening, asking questions, or being vulnerable.
- To some, confidence can mean trusting yourself to say or do the right thing, whatever the circumstance or situation.
- Still at other times, confidence means making hard decisions that align with your values or the impact you seek.

I cannot underscore enough how showing up with confidence will change the game for you.

Personally, I feel it in my body.

I'm looser. I laugh more. I lean in when I talk to people. I more thoughtfully contribute to conversations.

When I think back to the company gathering I mentioned at the start of this chapter, the confidence I exuded caught the attention of a senior leader at my table, who asked, "Remind me, what part of the business are you from again?" That growing confidence allowed me to make a lighthearted joke as I introduced myself to a C-suite executive over dinner later that day. And when I boarded my flight back to NYC, I felt the shift. I had arrived at the event full of doubt and questioning why I was there. But I was leaving with a renewed sense of belonging. Knowing that I deserved my seat at the table and feeling excited for what was next.

En resumen

We are not our fears or perceived weaknesses. We serve our own interests best when we show up unapologetically and fearlessly. The time to embrace your confidence is now. Say no to whatever is holding you back from stepping boldly into this moment. Silence the voices in your head that whisper, "You're not enough" or "You're too much." When you feel like you're a fish out of water, breathe, then take a moment to reflect on how much you've grown and all that you've overcome. Every experience has prepared you for this moment. Now, summon your courage and step into the discomfort with confidence.

Here are some reflection questions to help you explore your relationship with confidence and discover how you can show up in ways that align with your true intentions:

1. When have you shown up lacking confidence and how did it impact you?

   _____

   _____

   _____

   _____

2. What fears or limiting beliefs do you need to release to move forward?

   _____

   _____

   _____

   _____

3. What immediate changes can you make to show up with more confidence?

_____

_____

_____

_____

4. What longer-term adjustments can you make to cultivate lasting confidence?

_____

_____

_____

_____

CHAPTER 3

SAVE THE DRAMA FOR YOUR MAMA

"Santo que no me quiere, con no rezarle basta."[5]

---

[5] This refrán loosely translates to "If a saint doesn't love me, it's OK not to pray to them." What the refrán is really saying is that we're not for everyone and that's OK. We can give ourselves permission to move on when someone doesn't reciprocate the time or energy we're putting into the relationship. Knowing when to walk away is the key message of this refrán.

My mom said this saying a lot while I was growing up and I never quite understood the meaning. Growing up Catholic made it extra confusing for me. But I think I get it now. This saying is all about not seeking validation from others. It's about knowing when to let go, cut your losses, and move forward with confidence. When you reclaim your time and energy, you take control of your path, focusing on what truly serves your growth and well-being.

There's a hard truth that every professional must come to terms with. We are not for everyone. Said differently, everyone will not like us or be rooting for us. I'm not gonna lie. That's a very harsh reality to accept. And I cannot tell you how much time and energy I invested over the years trying to get other people to like me, support my ideas, or invest in my future.

You see, I thought them not rooting for me was about me. And while it's true that our vibe or energy can be off-putting to some, I firmly believe that most times, this lack of love or appreciation by others is more a reflection of the other person and what they got going on.

Getting laid off and starting my own business proved to be an eye-opening experience for me. I got ghosted by folks that I considered colleagues and friends or was flat out rejected by others without cause or explanation.

When I started my business, I reached out to organizations I admired, offering to host panels and fireside chats for their members. This was content that I was offering for free in the spirit of partnership and community but often I got no response.

Later, I reached out to leaders whose organizational missions were very closely aligned with my own, asking to explore partnership opportunities. Mostly, I was completely ignored and sometimes flat out rejected. In fact, I remember writing an email to one such leader and getting a note back saying, "We are not looking for strategic partners right now" then watching as they announced several new partnerships over the next few months.

I was declined the opportunity to work at several Latinx-serving organizations for reasons that were never shared with me. I realize that I'm not always the perfect fit for every role, but it was disheartening to be dismissed by organizations whose very mission is to uplift and support Latinx professionals and entrepreneurs.

Real talk

This kind of thing can be frustrating. And yet, I've discovered there's very little I can do to change how people act or how situations play out.

Let me share a story with you. A time when I thought I had done something wrong only to find out that the situation had nothing to do with me.

I had just started a new job. And a few days in, I noticed that one of my colleagues was being very rude to me. Like being short when she answered questions. Or telling me she was "very busy" when I was trying to get her attention. Basically, being super dismissive.

The more she ignored me, the harder I tried to connect with her. I complimented her hair and outfit, invited her to coffee, etc. She became a bit more cordial, but she was still mostly giving me the cold shoulder. I was about a week or two in and I was like "How the heck did I manage to fuck up a work relationship this soon without even realizing it?" She had me tripping.

Then one day, another colleague of mine found her crying in the break room. Turns out she had gotten a bad review a few days or weeks before I started my job and she was being nasty to me because she thought I was there to "replace her." Qué qué????

Come on, now.

When I look back on that moment, I can't help but laugh at how much I obsessed over what I might have done to offend her, only to realize her behavior was shaped by a story she was telling herself.

The lesson I learned from this situation really stuck with me. It taught me to focus on how *I* show up. So long as I'm treating others with kindness and respect, I've learned not to take *their* actions toward me personally. This mindset allows me to show up as my true self, focusing on building real, meaningful relationships, and staying clear of the drama.

No cosign needed

I need you to pay attention because I'm about to rock your world. I want to start by reminding you that you don't need anyone to cosign how you show up. It's natural to want approval from other people as you walk through the world, but let's be honest, that's not realistic. Owning your narrative is going to require that you stop looking to others to validate you and your choices.

Stop chasing their approval.

I spent a long time hoping someone in my industry would mentor me, validate how I was showing up, and advocate for me when I wasn't in the room. But that moment never came. If someone does that for you, recognize it for what it is: an act of kindness and generosity. Make sure to show gratitude for their support. However, most people will be too invested in their own thing to be worrying about you. Because of this, we must learn to let go of unrealistic expectations that don't serve us.

We are not for everyone

We are not for everyone and that's OK. Really. Like I said before, most of the time I don't even think it's about us. People are either worried about their own future, dealing with a personal crisis, or focused on their own growth and challenges. It's usually about them and not you. The less you make it about you, the easier it will be to cut your ties and move on.

Minda Harts, author of *The Memo*, reminds us that "We belong in every room we enter, but not every room deserves to have us." And it's true. Sometimes we try to force a square peg into a round hole and then get disappointed. I was like that a lot when I was younger. Knocking down doors and forcing my way into spaces. I don't do that anymore because I trust that what is meant for me will not be met with such strong resistance. The truth is that some spaces don't deserve us, and we must be OK with letting go and moving on.

Knowing when to move on

We'll know when we've overstayed our welcome. Folks will be dismissive. We may not get invited to meetings or put up for promotions. We may feel like we're being gaslit or lied to. There will be an excuse for everything that doesn't feel right or sit well with us. Those are all signs that it's time to go.

I remember working at a company for over seven years. Toward the end of my tenure there, they kept changing my manager. Then they gave me a special assignment that involved me going to a small town in the Midwest to work on a conversion for weeks at a time. At one point, I even got demoted and started reporting to someone who was formerly a peer. It got to be too much for me. I knew I had to leave because they did not appreciate the value I was bringing to the organization.

I ended up taking a job at a much more innovative company, making more money, with a lot more opportunities to travel to big cities and work with interesting customers. I may have overstayed my welcome by a year or two at my old job, but in the end, I did OK. I was able to improve my career trajectory by a lot with the move I made. It set me up for future roles. But more importantly, I learned that it's OK to make moves when I am no longer valued or appreciated.

So, take notice. If you're no longer being heard, if people are becoming unresponsive, or if it's clear that your value and contributions are going underappreciated, it might be time to move on. Don't take it personally—it's not always about you.

I want to remind you that you are the pilot of your own career, and it's important to stay alert to the bumps you experience along the way. Make the necessary adjustments to chart a smoother route when needed. You won't always have someone there to nudge you or tell you it's time to make a move or a change. Most of the time, you'll have to trust yourself and your instincts.

Trusting your inner voice

It takes time to learn how to trust your instincts. I'm an anxious person by nature so my body usually tells me when something doesn't feel right. I either get that feeling in the pit of my stomach or my mind starts replaying conversations, picking up on signs that something might be off.

Years ago, I had just started working at a tech company. About six months in, a colleague who started a few months before me got promoted. I asked them what they had done for this to happen. "Nothing," they said. "I found out during my annual review." Sweet, I thought. I've been doing a great job and consistently meeting my numbers so maybe I'll get promoted next cycle.

The next cycle came and went, and I got no promotion. I debated whether to ask my manager about it. Finally, I asked whether I had been considered for promotion. "No," they said. "Because we never talked about it."

I share this story all the time. With friends, in community spaces, but especially when talking to women and employees of color. This situation truly changed my life because it forced me to do things differently:

- I advocated for myself more in the workplace.
- I set up one-on-one meetings with my manager to talk about my professional goals.
- I kept a running list of achievements that I used as "receipts."
- I got managers to be transparent with me on the actual timelines for promotions and raises.
- I refused to ever again be caught off guard during a promotion cycle.

As a young professional, I would take whatever was given to me and say thank you. Along the way, I learned that if you don't ask, you don't get. Real talk. There's so much more waiting for us if we're bold enough to ask and determined enough to go after it.

A bit about boundaries

I can't end this chapter without talking about the most important self-preservation tool of all: boundaries. We must learn how to set them and honor them.

To illustrate boundaries, I must go back to a job I held that required me to be at a physical work location each day. In addition, that job required me to attend off-site meetings and go to our main office from time to time. None of these physical spaces were near each other so I was taking trains and buses to get from place to place.

After several months of this, I decided that it was not sustainable to keep up with this schedule. So, I decided that whenever I was off-site, I would go home after my meeting, instead of trying to go back to my main work site and run myself ragged. I didn't ask anyone for permission to do this. I didn't try to justify it. I just did it. I decided that my health and wellness came first and took it upon myself to do what was needed to honor that.

Boundaries are a two-step thing. First, I made the decision that the situation wasn't working for me and recognized that I had agency to change my circumstances. Next, I had to honor that choice each time I found myself feeling guilty for not "going back to work."

Don't get it twisted. I wasn't taking the time off. Not at all. I just decided that I would go home, answer emails during my travel time, and then be back at a decent hour to enjoy a nice dinner and evening of rest.

In the end, I think I did a better job because I was not run-down, and in turn, I could be kinder to my colleagues. I also made sure to tell my subordinates that they could feel free to do the same whenever they found themselves off-site. "You don't have to come back to work if you don't have a good reason to," I told them. My boundaries expanded because I wasn't just upholding them for myself, I was also ensuring that others made smart choices for themselves. Every person on my team became an extension of the boundary I had set, amplifying its impact. This was a valuable leadership lesson. I realized how much modeling positive behavior gave others permission to do the same.

Looking back, trusting myself was key to how I showed up in that role.

Boundaries and familia

Setting boundaries can be tricky for people. Perhaps even more for Latinas with parents and families who have high expectations.

I remember when I first graduated from college and moved to New Jersey. I would visit my mom in Queens every Saturday, without fail. The only exception was if I had to work. Work was a legit reason to not show up for family. Otherwise, I felt guilty AF for missing that time with my mom.

Over time, that changed. I once hosted a party on a Friday night so it was not realistic for me to get up at the crack of dawn for a two-hour drive to Queens. To my surprise, my mom actually didn't push back. She wanted me to have fun and hang out with friends. I was shocked to discover that the high expectations were mostly coming from me. WTAF!

This experience taught me I had the agency to set and honor boundaries as they related to my family just like I had the agency to draw the line in work situations. Yes, it might be harder to say no to Mami but sometimes it still needs to be done.

We must know when it's time to walk away, keep it moving, set our limits, or just say no. To do so is an act of self-love. You won't always get it perfectly right, but this is definitely one of those cases where practice makes perfect.

En resumen

Bottom line: trust yourself. Reclaim your power. Move forward with confidence. Choose peace as you determine where to focus your time and energy. It's important to know what matters to you because it will serve as a compass for the journey ahead.

Consider this: wherever you go, you take yourself with you. So why not bring the version of yourself that advocates for you, shows up for you, and makes decisions that serve your best interests? I'm telling you—start now. You'll thank yourself later.

And now, I invite you to reflect on these questions before you move to the next chapter:

1. Have you experienced being ghosted by others? How did it make you feel?

   _____

   _____

   _____

   _____

2. In what areas of your life are you still seeking approval or validation?

   _____

   _____

   _____

   _____

3. How do you remind yourself that the opinions of others are not a reflection of your self-worth?

_____

_____

_____

4. What would trusting yourself more look like?

_____

_____

_____

_____

CHAPTER 4

DESCUBRIENDO YOUR WHY

"El que busca, encuentra."[6]

---

[6]This refrán loosely translates to "The one who seeks, finds." Kind of like "Seek and you shall find." This refrán is highlighting the idea that persistence and effort will lead to discovery and success. Having determination and being proactive are the key messages of this refrán.

"That experience felt like church."

That was the feedback I got following a women's Employee Resource Group (ERG) event at a company where I worked. By all measures, that was a very big compliment.

At the time, I was the co-lead for an ERG event that was meant to show a rising ERG leader the best practices around member activation, partnering with the business, and collaborating with other ERGs.

A friend of a friend, who ran a local nonprofit, asked if our company would be willing to host an event for the girls in their program. Without hesitation, I accepted. I was always trying to find ways to sprinkle in purpose and impact into my workday.

As we got to planning, so many incredible ideas were coming up.

Let's get our senior leader involved in welcoming the girls and buying lunch.

Let's bring a senior woman leader to vulnerably share their own difficult beginnings and talk about how they overcame challenges to get to where they are now.

Let's do a fashion show that illustrates the dos and don'ts of corporate attire.

Let's gift all the girls a journal.

The list went on and on.

What started as a spark of an idea turned into a full day of learning and fun, engaging many of our employees—not just ERG members. One senior leader even purchased her favorite childhood book and gifted it to each one of the girls because she knew the power reading could have in helping the girls see past their current reality and dream of a better future.

At our prep meeting on the eve of the event, I reminded everyone that this was not just another work function. "We have an opportunity to make a real difference for these girls," I shared. "I want you to bring your heart to the day. I want you to really see these girls and make them feel valued and appreciated."

At the end of the event, after we took group photos, we gathered in a big circle and held hands. It was the end of our precious time together and it was sadly time to say goodbye. It was on me, as the senior co-lead, to send off our guests with some powerful parting words. I don't remember exactly what I said. All I know is that my voice cracked, and I cried as I spoke. I remember that other people around me were crying too. After my short speech, we hugged the girls, and we hugged each other. Mission accomplished: we filled the event with love and compassion, sending our guests off feeling truly seen and valued.

And that's how I discovered my purpose.

I don't know if I realized it in the moment, but looking back, it was so clear.

I'm here to make the world a better place by helping others feel truly valued and appreciated.

My purpose is to empower those who are often overlooked, teaching them the skills they need to thrive and succeed in a world that sometimes makes it hard for them to let their light shine.

BOOM!

Clarity is key and it will come when you least expect it. You know how they say you'll meet your life partner when you are not looking to meet them? It's kind of like that. For me, just doing the things I loved, that made my heart sing, allowed me to discover my higher purpose. I was open to receiving this important message from the Universe and I invite you to be too. When you don't have any expectations, you might just be pleasantly surprised at what you discover.

Your gifts

I walked around for a long time not quite knowing what my gifts were or how to put them to use. I knew I had a heart for service because I was always volunteering. When I was in college, I was a Big Sister. I also volunteered to go on a service trip during spring break. At work, I was part of a community service affinity group. We raised money for charity and came up with ways for other employees to donate their time and talent too. As part of a mentoring program, I organized a day of service where we spent meaningful time bonding with children while teaching them the essentials of personal finance. I hosted an annual holiday party at the local hospital and signed up employees to work shifts and donate presents. I was the lead for my company's partnership with Big Brothers Big Sisters. I volunteered at a children's hospital on the weekends and would bring coffee and tea to parents who were staying with their children in the NICU.

But I didn't really find my calling until I moved to Florida for work. I was relocated to Central Florida back in 2012. I remember driving my car down to Virginia to be loaded onto the train that would take me the rest of the way. The movie *Breakfast at Tiffany's* was playing on the train as I cried about whether I was making the right decision. I had lost my mom back in 2008 and my sister in 2011. I was ready to live a life of purpose. I didn't know how much longer I would be on this earth, but I knew I wanted to make my time count.

So, I joined a group at my local parish called JustFaith. This wasn't just any group, it was a nine-month commitment to meet weekly, do work in the community, and to otherwise share our journey with each other. I went on this journey with a very special group of individuals who touched me in profound ways. We read a ton of books, watched videos, connected with community organizations, all with the goal of understanding the relationship between our faith and social justice. It was a powerful experience. So much so that I decided I might want to go on mission.

Before heading to Bolivia for two years, I did a couple of test runs.

I went to Haiti for a week and loved it. I was inspired by the enthusiasm of the next generation, moved by the faith of the people, and humbled by the generosity of a country that had very little. My trip to Haiti awakened my call to mission. It was there that I was first called a missioner.

A few months later, I took another mission trip, this time to El Salvador. I visited missioners at their ministry sites: One missioner worked at an afterschool program with children, another hosted a soymilk program to bring more nutritional beverage options to the community, and another worked with HIV and AIDS patients. I marveled at the work that was being done and the joy I saw in the faces of every missioner we met. They really seemed to enjoy the work they were doing. It was inspiring to me. It gave me hope there were ways I could put my purpose to good use.

I'll be talking more about my time in Bolivia as a missioner in a future chapter. What I want to leave you with here is that my purpose was right in front of me the whole time. THE WHOLE TIME. I just couldn't see it because I was so busy in my corporate bubble. Once I created space to consider where I fit in and what superpower lived deep within me, I was able to see it so clearly.

If you're still struggling to understand your purpose, allow me to give you some practical tips.

1. **You can make a list of the common threads in the activities you love.** If I did this, I would discover that I'm always finding ways to make other people feel included, heard, and valued.
2. **You can ask friends and family to share what they observe.** Be careful with this one. Everyone may have good intentions but not everyone will give this question the thoughtfulness it requires. Choose people in your life you deeply trust and who will take the time to seriously consider their response.
3. **Keep a running inventory.** This practice can be incredibly insightful, as it helps you identify patterns and connections. By listing activities you love, moments that energize you, and work you'd engage in without reward or recognition, you can uncover meaningful clues about where your true purpose lies.

Finding alignment

When you have found your purpose and discovered your why, you'll know it. You'll experience a sense of alignment. "What's that," you ask?

It's the feeling that everything happens as it should. It's a sense of flow. Personal alignment will feel like your decisions are deeply rooted in your beliefs. Professional alignment will feel like your work reflects your values. And relational alignment will feel like your connections are authentic and mutual.

I think the biggest sign that you are living and walking in your purpose is the joy you will get out of your work, interactions, and projects. Everything will feel connected because it shares the same foundation.

Right now, my work is focused on supporting ERG leaders and creating opportunities for them to shine in every space they occupy. I give talks, write essays, and lead workshops that are aligned with this underlying purpose.

My volunteer work in organizations such as Ellevate Network and Lean In Latinas is rooted in the same common thread. To support our members on their professional journeys. Create brave spaces for them to learn and grow. Send them out into the world knowing they can achieve whatever they set their hearts to.

My circle of friends and colleagues reflects my values. I automatically am drawn to like-minded individuals who selflessly give of themselves to make the path easier for others. Most people in my network are not wealthy, but they are rich in kindness and generosity. They are not doing the work for themselves but for the greater good. Like attracts like and my network is truly a reflection of me. As my mom always used to say, "Dime con quién andas y te diré quien eres."[7] The company we keep says a lot about us. Choose wisely.

---

[7] This refrán loosely translates to "Tell me who you spend time with, and I will tell you who you are." Exercising good judgement in the company we keep is the key message of this refrán.

Taking action

In this chapter, we've talked about discovering our purpose, recognizing our unique gifts, and the value of perfect alignment. I want to close out the chapter by saying that if you've done all of this but don't put your purpose to work, you've missed the plot.

Purpose without action is nothing. You must, I repeat, YOU MUST put your purpose into action to step into your power. This could be scary for some of us. I get it. I left a twenty-year career in corporate to go be a missioner in Bolivia and work with incarcerated women. Some people were like "Are you crazy?" Shit, I cannot tell you how many days I would wake up and tell myself, "No way, you are not doing this, this is way too disruptive." But then I would think about how fun it would be to live in my purpose and how great it would feel to live according to my values, and I would fall in love with the idea all over again.

Fortunately, living in your purpose will not necessarily require you to quit your job and move overseas. It might. But in all likelihood, there are ways for you to incorporate your purpose into any job you have right now. The key is to align your work with your passions. If that's missing from your current 9–5, a volunteer gig might be the perfect opportunity to tap into what truly lights you up and brings you joy. Your purpose is right there, sis. Claim it.

For twenty years, I raised my hand to work with ERGs because I knew they were the kind of spaces that allowed me to live in my purpose. I could support other employees, make them feel seen, and give allies a way to support those efforts. Eventually, I chose a career that allowed me to do this as my day job and not just a side hustle. But it took a long time. What I appreciate about myself is that I always recognized how much ERG work nourished a part of me, so I made it a priority alongside my day-to-day responsibilities.

I couldn't have known this about myself if I didn't make time to *notice* what brought me joy and fulfillment. Finding your purpose requires a lot of self-awareness.

I also wouldn't have known this about myself if I didn't *quiet the noise* around me. Going on retreats and spending time in silence and reflection were important steps in my transformation.

All this wouldn't have mattered if I wasn't *brave enough* to move toward greater alignment. Reading about the lives of fearless leaders like Martin Luther King Jr., Dolores Huerta, and Oscar Romero was instrumental for me. They showed me that while living a life of purpose isn't always easy, or convenient, there is deep joy and peace in doing the work you are meant for.

Once you discover what makes your heart sing, lean in and let go! Enjoy the ride. Do more of it. Find new and creative ways to show up. Partner with others on a similar mission. Find your people and go all in.

En resumen

Your why is what gets you up in the morning and gets you going. It's what makes you feel in the flow. It's what brings a smile to your face and what you can do effortlessly. It's not work. It's your purpose. Your why is the thing you would do for free.

Align as much of your life to your why to live a fulfilling life. Surround yourself with others whose values and purpose are aligned with yours. These are your people. Spend as much time as you can with them. They will remind you of who you are and why you do what you do when things get tough. They will lift you up, be a shoulder to cry on, and be your biggest cheerleaders.

And now, I leave you with a few questions to ponder as you think about your why:

1. Have you ever had a transformative experience that helped clarify your purpose?

   _____

   _____

   _____

2. What common threads or patterns do you notice in the work, hobbies, or activities that bring you joy?

   _____

   _____

   _____

3. What aspects of your life feel most aligned with who you are and what you value?

   _____

   _____

   _____

4. What small steps can you take today to align more of your life with your "why"?

_____

_____

_____

_____

CHAPTER 5

FIRST, BUILD COMUNIDAD

"Hoy por ti, mañana por mi."[8]

---

[8]This refrán loosely translates to "Today for you, tomorrow for me." This refrán emphasizes community, kindness, and the belief that we all benefit when we support one another. I believe what this refrán represents very deeply in my heart. Supporting each other is the key message of this refrán.

"Kiki and I will bring a cake," I said. "Do we need anything else?" I was in San Sebastian Mujeres in Cochabamba, Bolivia where I volunteered as a Francian lay missioner during 2014 and 2015. I was talking to some of the women I visited in prison each week. We were planning a birthday party for one of the women in the group. C was cooking (she was a chef when she wasn't in prison), E was making a card we could all sign, and Kiki and I would pick up the cake for the party. We were all set for the birthday bash.

I must tell you that when I first signed up to go on mission, and volunteer at a prison, I was not envisioning that I would be planning birthday parties for the women or calling them friends. But friends we were. Those women got to know me quite well. They knew when I was not feeling my best, when I was sad, when I was homesick, and when I was heartbroken. They got to know me just like any other friend would.

We spent lots of time together. I started a women's prayer group (which was really a support group), I practiced English with them (which just turned out to be fun hangout time more than anything else), and I volunteered at the hair salon (which was run by another missioner). We spent a lot of time together and really showed up for each other.

I guess it was this last part that surprised me. When I said yes to "ministry of presence," I kind of thought I would be the one showing up for them. I never, ever expected that they would offer me their friendship in return. This mutual friendship that evolved over time was equal parts life-giving and surprising to me. I found myself being held by the women when I needed it the most. I will never forget the kindness offered to me by people who were undoubtedly experiencing some of their worst moments of their lives.

You wouldn't know it, though, from how we interacted. Take the time my Aunt Lucy was visiting from Puerto Rico. I told the women for weeks that my aunt was going to come and that she would be cooking an authentic Puerto Rican meal for them. They were very excited and welcomed Lucy into the space with open arms. C was Lucy's sous chef during her visit and helped her prepare the meal. She was taking notes because the plan was that she would try making the food again after Lucy's visit. If I remember correctly, Lucy made arroz con gandules with costillitas (a.k.a. yellow rice with pigeon peas and braised ribs).

Funny story. When we arrived at the prison, the guard wasn't quite sure what we were up to. So, we struck a deal with her: We'd bring her a plate of food in return for her letting us in with a pot, two cans of peas, and a bag of rice.

While we ate, Lucy was in the hot seat and the women could ask her anything. They asked about her first love, being a mother, the aging process, and so much more. I remember Lucy shared a very personal story from her first marriage which the women really seemed to relate to. It was such an amazing day!

There was another time I came to visit after the holidays so maybe we hadn't seen each other in a few weeks. We had a lot of catching up to do! We were sitting at a table talking, laughing, and really enjoying one another's company. We may have been enjoying it too much because one of the guards came over and asked me why I was there. I told her I was a missioner who visited the women a few times a week. She reminded me that I was not there to have fun, and neither were the women, and then she asked me to leave. I felt so bad because I thought my friends would get punished after I left. I called a few hours later and my friend E assured me that they were fine and that whole episode was just for show.

I really ended up developing a very special place in my heart for these women who welcomed me into their space and lives in such a kind and generous way. I was not once scared or anxious about being at the prison because I knew I was loved and appreciated.

One day, one of the women even told me, "We love the days when you visit us because it makes us forget we're in prison." I will forever be grateful for what she shared with me. Most of us aren't lucky enough to get that kind of feedback. I took what she said as a gift. One of the many gifts that I received from my friends at San Sebastian Mujeres.

When I think back to that time, what stands out most is how life-giving the community was. It became that way for a variety of reasons:

- **Shared vulnerability:** Each of us, including me, was going through an extraordinary experience that left us open and willing to embrace something new.
- **Mutual support:** We saw in one another what we deeply needed: support, encouragement, and non-judgment.

- **Trust:** We took the time to build a solid foundation for our friendships, rooted in trust.
- **Respect:** We honored our time together by respecting our shared values and community agreements, i.e., "leave your drama at the door."
- **Adaptability:** Our community responded with grace to the addition of new members (sometimes almost weekly) and the departure of others, as some people left the prison.

After returning to the United States, I worked at an elementary school in the South Bronx where I served as the Community School Director. I was charged with engaging families and providing services to the school community. One of the first things I did was create a weekly parent support space we called Coffee Time. I used many of the same principles to build this community.

And I have used these principles repeatedly wherever I see an opportunity to use them. Because what I've discovered is that community can be intentionally built, organically formed, or often, a combination of the two. How I've seen it work best is that you start a group with a lot of intentionality. Then, you see the magic of the group start to take over. At that point, you can let go and watch the community grow. You'll know it when it's happening because you'll feel safe, supported, seen, heard, valued, and appreciated. Yes, all the things. You'll feel them all when community building is at work.

Building comunidad from the ground up

Let me take a moment here to share that while a loving community can feel like magic, getting there requires hard work.

As an example, for there to be shared vulnerability, it requires a brave soul to be vulnerable first and model the behavior for everyone else. It can't be something you preach. It must be something you are willing to do consistently.

Likewise, if you want to feel supported, you need to demonstrate what support looks like so folks know how to show up for one another. I remember when someone was going through a difficult moment at the prison, we took the time to acknowledge what they were dealing with. We created space for community members when they needed it. People came to trust that when they needed support, they could ask for it. That's a powerful norm to establish in a community.

Building trust ain't easy. Especially because once it's broken, it's very hard to build back up. And yet, I was able to create a trusted, safe space in a prison because I challenged the women to trust each other during our time together, and they bravely rose to the occasion. One key ingredient to building trust was simply showing up for the women week in and week out. They trusted I would be there for them because I said I would, and I followed through. That simple action inspired them to then show up for me and each other with respect and appreciation.

Respect in community comes from the top. When, as a leader, I show care for every single member, I am modeling the behavior I expect from others. It's really important to call out anyone who is not contributing to a positive group dynamic. People need to understand what's acceptable and what's not. I used to tell women in my support group that if they didn't respect each other in the space, they would not be welcome.

But I'm no fool. I understood that fostering a thriving community required both clear boundaries AND the flexibility to meet people where they were. As an example, while it's natural to feel sadness when members move on, the community must continue to grow and evolve. My approach, in a situation like this, is to acknowledge the loss while highlighting my gratitude for the time they spent with us and for those who remain. True community shouldn't rely on just one person but on the strength of the entire group. A good leader ensures there are ways for the community to thrive, with or without their presence. Things you can do as a leader are to build up other members, shine the light on emerging leaders, and help others see your vision for the group so that it can live on even after you're gone.

How to find your people

My primary advice on finding your people would be to use your values and purpose to identify communities that align with who you are or celebrate a shared identity. As an example, I love to build up and empower Latinas, so I joined and worked my way up the leadership ranks of Lean In Latinas. Once I joined the community and discovered how aligned it was with my values, it was clear that I should "lean in" (pun intended) more because this group is very focused on the things that matter to me.

On the other hand, I've joined groups that initially felt aligned with my purpose, only to realize over time that they weren't. It happens. Groups evolve, priorities shift, and sometimes leadership struggles to build trust or foster respect among members. When these foundational principles erode, a group may no longer feel safe or aligned with you. That might be a sign to seek a new space that truly fills and fuels you.

At times, you may know exactly what you're looking for but struggle to find a community that aligns with your priorities. That could be your opportunity to create and design a new group for people like you. For me, building a community from scratch is exciting. You get to shape its mission, vision, and purpose just the way you like. And the most rewarding part? Over time, as people connect with it, the community takes on a life of its own.

Abundance mindset as the foundation

I'm often asked why I like community building so much (yes, I very much consider community part of my personal brand). It comes down to a core belief of mine: there are enough resources and opportunities for everyone to succeed. I firmly believe that when one of us wins, we all win. And because of this deep-rooted belief, I can give everything I got to another community member, knowing that there is still plenty left in the kitty for me to receive. I am genuinely happy when you succeed, and my hope is that you will be equally as happy when it's my turn.

Not everyone thinks this way. It's sad but it's true. I have had many folks feel threatened by me or envious of my success. I could tell by the way I'm treated or even by the things people say. I remember this one time winning an award at work and having my own team members treat me very badly after the award was announced. They questioned me winning the award so much (to my face and behind my back) that I started to question whether I deserved it at all. I ended up asking my manager why I had received the award, and after they shared why I had earned it, I felt better about why I got it, yet it still didn't change how people on my own team treated me.

Needless to say, those were not my people. Your people will always be happy to see you winning and they will be the first ones there to celebrate with you. I find that I can convert some people into an abundance mindset by demonstrating my joy for them in their big moments. Sometimes, I'm able to help people see that life isn't a "if you win, then I lose" scenario. Instead, it's about getting that "there's enough for both of us to win and celebrate each other's success."

Pouring into others

Pouring into others is where it's at. Give praise freely, keeping in mind that the spotlight isn't always meant to shine on you. Find strengths in others and remind them of their superpowers whenever you can. Give people shout-outs in private and in public. Mentor and coach junior people. Help others find their path in a kind way.

Listen and hold space for others. Accompany people as they discover their own mission and purpose. Share experiences and lessons you've learned along your journey. Recognize boundaries and reserve judgement unless specifically asked.

Offer words of encouragement and support. Remind people of who they are. You are a badass. You are a chingona. You are una mujer poderosa. Don't hold back when it comes to this part. This is what people need most and if you're in the position to reignite someone else's flame, do it. We will never regret being there for someone in their time of need.

Keep in mind that some people will not ask for help or support. Sometimes I'm one of those people. I want to be strong and asking others for their support doesn't come easy to me. Therefore, just give. You may or may not get the gift of knowing what your words meant to another. But that doesn't matter. The point is to give selflessly and often.

Amplify one another

Spotlight another at every turn. Amplify a win, celebrate achievements, and otherwise lift one another. Uplift others regardless of whether they're more seasoned or experienced than you. That part doesn't matter. I equally amplify the work of a more junior person in the same way I would spotlight someone who is further along on their journey than I am. Age, level, education, etc. don't matter when you're celebrating another. Greatness and excellence can truly come from anyone at any age or stage. Pay attention.

Believe in the law of reciprocity which says that when you show others kindness and support, it will eventually come back to you in some form. Not that this would be your main reason for being kind. But rather that you understand there is a flow at play. Today it's someone else's turn and tomorrow might be your time to shine. If you believe this, it's very easy to show others support and encouragement when it's their time. As a reminder, there's enough for all of us. If you believe that, you can be happy for others. Period.

En resumen

We all need community. To feel loved, to feel supported, and to feel seen. You can and should choose the community that fills your cup. I've been lucky enough to find community in so many beautiful spaces.

Be open to learning from others and growing together. Laughter, joy, and authenticity are keys to any community. So is holding space for grief, disappointment, and sadness. And don't forget about the principles we talked about earlier in this chapter: shared vulnerability, mutual support, trust, respect, and last but not least, adaptability.

Once you get the hang of it, you will find it easy to identify your people and the spaces you can call home. Sometimes home will be an ERG. Other times it will be a Latinx-serving nonprofit created to lift our community. And still other times, it will be a powerful coalition of ambitious and supportive women who choose to learn from each other, share ideas, and grow together.

My hope is that you find your people, your community, and your home. And that you pour into it with love and compassion for the people around you. Remember, in a true community, there is no gatekeeping, just love.

As we wrap up this section, I would like to offer you some questions to reflect on:

1. How and when have you experienced community in your own life?

   _____

   _____

   _____

   _____

2. How does adopting an abundance mindset change the way you view success in the context of community?

_____

_____

_____

3. How can your unique strengths or experiences contribute to building a stronger, more supportive community?

_____

_____

_____

4. Reflect on the law of reciprocity. Can you think of a time when kindness or support came back to you in an unexpected way?

_____

_____

_____

_____

CHAPTER 6

SELF-CARE, SIEMPRE

"Quien bien se cuida, bien vive."⁹

---

⁹This refrán loosely translates to "Those who take good care of themselves live well." The refrán conveys the idea that self-care is essential for living a good, healthy, and fulfilling life. Self-care as the foundation for a happy life is the key message of this refrán.

The migraines were back. I was getting them every few weeks since the middle of October. They were quite disruptive, especially since I just started my new role over the summer, and I was getting to the point where I really wanted my workdays to end so I didn't have to sit in front of a computer anymore.

On this particular day, I was supposed to meet with my direct and dotted line managers. We had instituted joint meetings once a month because it was becoming increasingly clear that we were not all on the same page. I was hired with the understanding that my role was to advocate for the folks I supported but was just coming to realize that maybe that wasn't everyone's priority. It was tearing me apart, if I'm honest, because I pride myself in being a top performer and was struggling to find a way to thrive in this new position. My dotted line manager had recently asked me if "I was *sure* I wanted to be in this role" which, I'm not gonna lie, was one of the weirdest questions I've ever been asked by a senior leader. It was a sign to me that something wasn't right, and I was trying my hardest to get us all to common ground.

I had prepared an agenda for the call, which I shared in advance. I also sent them a chat message ahead of our call to let them know I was not feeling great. I didn't send the message with the intention of canceling the call but more to get them to be a little gentler with me given my current state.

Anyways, my dotted line manager shot back a message saying, "Do we need to reschedule?" "No," I said. "I should be fine." And I pushed through the meeting. On that call, she was mean and rude to me. At one point even saying, "That is on a need-to-know basis and you don't need to know." That was a lot coming from a senior leader. I left the meeting feeling like I was going to throw up.

The current situation was especially frustrating because I had just finished recovering from intense chest pain, which took months of physical therapy to resolve. The pain in my chest sometimes got so awful that I would adjust my camera so I could have a heating pad on my chest during customer calls. I avoided telling anyone about it—especially my manager at the time—since we were focused on securing an early promotion for me to correct the mis-leveling that occurred when I was hired.

As you can see there was a common thread here. All the drama at work seemed to be manifesting itself through my body. And it wasn't good.

Thankfully, I was able to move on from that awful role in just a few short months, although I didn't know it at the time of the call. I'm grateful that I finally got a break from being in a situation where no one was happy. I was not happy that my role did not allow me to speak out on behalf of the employees I supported. And leadership clearly thought I was a lost cause in the art of "getting with the program." They just wanted me to do what I was told. Looking back, if that's what they were looking for all along, I'm not sure why they hired me.

I am a team player just like the next person, but I will not sit back and watch folks be treated unfairly and do nothing.

After I moved away from the position, I took a bit of a sabbatical before moving on to my next role. I'm happy to report the headaches went away and never came back. When I reflect on my experience, I can conclude without hesitation that stress is not just something people talk about. It really and truly can affect your physical and mental health, and it did for me.

Through this horrible experience, I learned to better manage my health and wellness. I saw the direct relationship that an unhealthy work situation was having on me. I vowed to do better. To advocate for myself. To choose me.

Throughout this book so far, we've been talking about stepping into our power and doing amazing shit. I'm here to tell you that taking control of your health and wellness is a powerful way to reclaim your energy, purpose, and strength. So powerful that when you make yourself a priority, you are in fact not only claiming your own power, but you are modeling for others how they can show up too. This modeling of behavior, which I talked about in an earlier chapter, is key. Because we are leaders and people are not only listening to what we say but also watching what we do. Anyone can say, "My health comes first," but not everyone is willing to make the sacrifices that are needed to live that truth.

Self-advocacy in action

You know how some people can't see at night? I'm one of those people. Driving at night wasn't always an issue for me because I mostly worked near where I lived or relied on public transportation to get me from point A to point B. Also, the problem got progressively worse over the years.

I once worked for a company that merged with another company. The company I originally worked for was walking distance from my home. The new company was a ninety-minute drive on busy highways. When the companies merged, I was told I should find ways to work out of the new office, since all of my management team was now working there.

It was a nonstarter for me. It was easy to see why I would choose a ten-minute walk to work as opposed to a ninety-minute drive. However, as the weeks and months went by, I saw that I was getting screwed in the reorg and that I would have to show my face if I wanted to maintain my current role and level. So, I started to drive in to the new office a few times a week. Given my issue with not being able to see at night, I would drive in early and leave early so I could get home before dark. People noticed.

At one point, folks started to approach me and say, "Must be nice to have banker's hours" to which I would promptly reply, "I can't see at night so in order to avoid getting into a bad accident, I choose to leave while it's still daylight." Most people stopped making comments after I told them that. But I didn't really care, tbh. I was choosing my safety, and I stood by my choice. I ended up getting a demotion on that team. Mostly because my manager didn't advocate for me but also because I wasn't well-known by the new leaders, and my priorities were often misunderstood or frowned upon.

I don't tell you this story to scare you because I still want you to choose yourself first. Not everyone is going to like or agree with your decisions, but that's on them. You need to be thoughtful and intentional about how you want to show up and then forget about what people say. I stand by my decision to leave work early all day long.

That job, and keeping my role, was not worth putting myself in physical danger. PERIOD.

You're probably wondering what happened next. I stayed in the demoted role for a few more months but I think you already know that I'm not about that life. I find ways to propel myself forward no matter what. So I ended up advocating for myself and transferring to an entirely new team at the company. The new job was a step up for me, offering greater visibility and more customer face time.

A part of me has always known that things will work out if I make decisions rooted in good faith and personal integrity. This belief helped me dismiss any judgments from colleagues. I knew I was prioritizing my self-care and if my organization didn't value or respect that choice, it was up to me to decide my next move.

Rest and restoration

Rest is one of my favorite things. Not sleep, per se, but just getting to do nothing. Maybe go for a walk and listen to a podcast. Or sit in front of my laptop and stream a show. Or maybe just head over to a park and read. Rest means I get to do something I enjoy that makes me feel relaxed and not stressed. I mentioned earlier in this book that I consider myself to be an anxious person. I deal with this in a lot of ways: I keep my calendar organized, I give myself plenty of time to complete a task, and I don't overcommit myself. But one of my favorite things to do is just kick back and unwind.

Over the years, I've taken a lot of rest-filled vacations. Mostly I don't vacation at a beach resort or sip margaritas by the pool. That is not relaxing to me at all. I had to learn that over the years because for most people, that's what works.

I like taking two types of vacations.

For many years, I've taken vacations that involve resting my physical body (think restorative yoga) and eating healthy meals. I've gone on yoga retreats in places like Italy and Bali. I even did this goddess bootcamp back in my forties and absolutely loved it. It was what a lot of people would consider a "hippie-dippie retreat" but I loved it so much because the focus was on my physical and spiritual wellness, and to me, that's what helps me to relax, get centered, and feel grounded.

The other kind of vacation I love is restful too but in a totally different way. The second type involves slow days filled with walking, exploring, taking pictures, and chance encounters. To me this is so much fun and relaxing. Not having anywhere to be, not feeling stressed about commitments or obligations, and just really getting to be present. I have discovered so much great street art on days like these. And places to eat. And fabulous shops. And awesome music venues. You get the idea. Losing track of time and getting to explore is super relaxing for me.

When I think of rest, I think of a great night's sleep; followed by nutritious meals; a slow, relaxing, unrushed day; more great food; interesting finds; and a cozy evening that leads to another great night of sleep.

I should probably stop here and say that vacations are great, but we can't wait until we have a vacation day or week to take care of ourselves. Rest and restoration are not optional. They are not rewards. They are things that our body and spirit require, and we must find ways to commit to them daily.

For me, protecting my peace is a big part of feeling restored. So is adopting practices that bring me back to center. I do this by walking two to three times a day, blocking out an hour for breakfast, lunch, and dinner each day, and taking Fridays off on most weeks to give myself even more time to do things that help me feel focused, creative, and grounded. I also limit my caffeine intake as much as possible, drink lots of water, eat nutritious meals, spend time outside, read before bed, keep my home cool at night (great for sleeping!), wear mostly cotton as that's what feels best on my skin, use natural products (i.e., deodorants, soap, shampoo, detergent, toothpaste), and keep an air purifier and humidifier in my home. There's probably more I can add to the list, but you get the idea. My body is my temple, and I treat myself like a fucking queen. Why not? I'm blessed enough to be able to afford to treat myself well and so I make it a priority to do so.

Sis, I want you to feel like a million bucks too! You deserve it. When you take care of yourself, you'll show up energized, focused, calm, and centered. You'll be ready to take on new challenges, feeling rested and balanced. You'll make smarter decisions, stay upbeat and positive, and draw in the people who truly align with you.

I want all of this for you. And I hope you do too!

What you eat and drink

I'm sure you've heard the phrase "You are what you eat," but have you ever stopped to think about what that means? I have.

I'll start off this section by saying that what I'm about to share is not meant to be a judgement call on you. Everyone has the agency to choose what they eat and put into their bodies. I have chosen to be extremely thoughtful on this front. Mostly because I have a sensitive stomach but also because I have noticed the difference it makes when I eat more nutritious meals. I have more energy, I think more clearly, and I just generally feel lighter.

Make the decisions that work for you. I want to encourage you to reflect on your current diet and to consider making some changes that might improve your overall health and wellness. Your future self will thank you for it.

So back to what I eat. I usually eat a gluten-free, dairy-free, refined-sugar-free diet and it works well for me. I cheat on very rare occasions and trust me when I tell you that my body knows the difference. I will either get a bad stomachache, feel bloated, or worse case, feel crappy for days at a time. So yeah, I mostly don't cheat because it isn't worth it.

My diet helps me to stay regular. This is important for me as I was one of those people that took fiber supplements for years. My diet and exercise regimen also help me to stay fit. I have been a size zero a few times in my life. That's not necessarily my goal, though. I mostly just want to feel strong and confident in my body as I move through the world.

I don't drink alcohol much these days. That was a decision I made for health reasons but one I happily stand by. Alcohol, at this point, does not agree with my body. And that's fine. I may decide to have a drink a few times a year but mostly I don't. It's not worth it to me.

These are the decisions that work for me. You might decide to make different choices based on your lifestyle and body. Again, what I hope for more than anything is that you listen to your own body and come up with strategies that will help you feel your best.

My health and wellness recipe

I would say that my recipe for health and wellness is made up of three key ingredients:

1. **Balance of movement and rest:** I love to walk. I also enjoy stretching. So, my movement regimen is mostly made up of

these two things. I also rest as much as I can. Sometimes this means getting a good night's sleep. Sometimes it means just slowing down and being more present.
2. **Diet and mindful eating habits:** I enjoy eating and find myself eating a meal or snacking most of the day. I usually have breakfast around 7 a.m. and dinner by 5 p.m. I don't eat anymore after that because I want to make sure everything I eat is fully digested before I go to bed. During the day, I snack on things like popcorn, nuts, and nutritious baked goods. I make my own berry jam fresh every week. I drink mostly water and tea. That's me and what works to keep me healthy and well.
3. **Fun:** This is the good stuff. My solo travel trips. My yoga retreats. My street art photography tours. Reading before bed each night. Daily cafecitos with a treat that I know won't upset my stomach. Massages and pedicures. You get the idea.

Your health and wellness recipe will probably not look like mine. We are all different and require different strategies to feel at the top of our game. Notice what works for you and incorporate more of that into your routine. Likewise, notice what sets you off, depletes your energy, or doesn't make you feel great, and do less of that. The ingredients you choose to include are up to you and will probably shift as your body and life circumstances change.

If coming up with your own recipe for success feels hard, consider this:

- You know yourself best. Trust your judgment over anyone else's advice on what you should or shouldn't be doing. After all, your self-care plan should be as unique as you are!

- Notice what sets you off or triggers you. Is there a way to reduce these experiences or moments?
- Notice what regulates and calms you. Can you do more of what makes you feel safe and well?
- Create a personalized self-care plan and commit to it. It doesn't need to be perfect to start. Do what works and adjust as needed!

En resumen

Make time to rest and restore. FULL STOP. Your body requires it. Your brain and spirit will appreciate it. Be mindful of the things you put into your body. Notice what makes you feel lighter, more focused, more clear-minded. Consider what a routine rooted in movement and rest might look like for you. I know I have the privilege of living alone, and I recognize that creating space for yourself can be tougher when you're juggling family responsibilities or sharing a home. Your routine doesn't have to look like mine. But I trust you will find one that works for you.

Why bother with all of this? Is it really necessary? I don't know about you but getting really bad migraines ain't it. Or worrying about getting into a car accident either. I choose myself daily because I want to be in an optimum place to show up for myself and others. Make whatever changes you feel are necessary for yourself, your family, and your overall well-being. Trust that when you feel your best, you will be able to do your best work.

Before we leave this chapter, I want to leave you some reflection questions to think about:

1. What health concerns are you currently facing and what changes would you like to make?

   _____
   _____
   _____
   _____

2. What's your current recipe for health and wellness? Is it helping you thrive?

   _____
   _____
   _____
   _____

3. What's one small change you can make today to enhance your wellness journey?

   _____
   _____
   _____
   _____

4. What other strategies can you explore to boost your health and well-being?

   _____

   _____

   _____

   _____

CHAPTER 7

MUJER, TAKE UP SPACE

"Camarón que duerme se lo lleva la corriente."[10]

[10]This refrán loosely translates to "The shrimp who sleeps will be washed away by the current." Yikes! I love it because it reminds me of the English phrase "Don't sleep on it." It's a call to action, urging us not to just go through the motions of life. Instead, we should choose our actions and behaviors intentionally and with purpose. Staying alert and being proactive are the key messages of this refrán.

"Make sure you meet with everyone ahead of the meeting. That's how you protect yourself from things going awry at the steering committee meeting. You need to have the meeting before the meeting. The pre-meeting."

I didn't always have the pre-meeting. Mostly because I thought they were dumb. You mean to tell me if I don't meet with you before a big meeting, you will use that as a license to publicly throw me under the bus?

Yup, pretty much.

I remember walking into a room filled with folks that I admired but really didn't know very well. They were part of the leadership team at the company where I worked. And full of bravado. Each one trying to outdo the next when it came to wielding their power and instilling fear in folks that never saw it coming.

They were polite to me. Mostly because my manager was one of them and she looked out for me. While they had no problem crossing me, they would think twice before crossing her.

I remember going into these steering committee meetings to defend the projects I was working on. I was always nervous about such meetings because I didn't know what to expect. I was fearful that someone would try to undermine me with an unexpected "gotcha" that I was not prepared for. Almost always, I would regret not having the pre-meetings my manager had warned me about.

So, did I come around to setting up these pre-meetings? Yes. Did I have to do it every time? No. Because, over time I learned that the pre-meetings were not about "providing context" so people better understood my project and related updates and requests. The meetings were all about recognizing the power and influence of the people in the room. They were about paying your respects and acknowledging their authority.

In time, I learned to look forward to these steering committee meetings. The situation hadn't changed. Instead, what changed was me. Instead of shrinking as I walked into these rooms, I was excited to share the work I was engaged in and how it was moving the needle. You see, as a program manager, I had developed some power and influence of my own.

I eventually learned that I didn't have to be nervous when I entered those rooms because I was doing impactful work and doing it well. When you're running big projects that will have a significant impact on the business, you have power. When you're executing those projects well, that gives you power too. And when you're one of the most knowledgeable people on those projects? Yup, you guessed it—you have power.

While folks still had the power to pull my budget, I was delivering the outcomes that made everyone in the room look good. The most important pre-meeting I needed was with myself so I could show up to these meetings prepared and backed by receipts. The rest took care of itself.

What did showing up with receipts look like? It meant documenting all my accomplishments. It meant showing how I was saving the company money. It meant outlining exactly how I would be spending extra budget dollars. It meant saving email threads where I raised important issues with colleagues. It meant tracking project risks in a document that I reviewed with senior leaders regularly. I basically dotted every "i" and crossed every "t" that I could find.

Bottom line: I was moving strategically and with intention.

I'm guessing you too have walked into rooms like the one I've described. Maybe it wasn't a steering committee meeting but it was a space where you had to defend your work and/or be questioned by folks with more seniority or power. If you don't have anyone advocating for you behind the scenes, these spaces can be scary for anyone, let alone a Woman of Color. Some people believe we don't belong in those spaces and will remind us of that at every turn. The fear is meant to keep us in our place. To remind us that they can ruin our reputation if they choose to. To signal who's in charge.

The dynamics in these rooms, while in some cases have gotten better, still need some serious reform. My guess is that the composition of who's in power isn't going to change any time soon. So where does that leave us?

It means the transformation needs to come from us. From inside us. We can reclaim our power. Need some inspiration to believe what I'm telling you? Read and process the words of Alice Walker who once said, "The most common way people give up their power is by thinking they don't have any."

And I, for one, am done giving my power away. I'm reclaiming that shit and hope you decide too as well.

Step into your power

Ever since I started my speaking career, my main talk has always been about self-advocacy and self-promotion. These are two extremely valuable tools to incorporate into how you show up at work, at home, and in life.

One of the ways you can step into your power is by finding your voice. This is not easy for everyone. Some people are shy. Others are introverted. And still others, fearful of the consequences of speaking out. People might not like you or agree with you. Others will attempt to silence you by using their power over you. Still others will try to turn the table and make you feel like the bad guy. I've seen and heard it all in my thirty-year career.

My favorite example of people turning the tables on me was the time my manager called me "disruptive" at team meetings. When I asked them to explain why, they said I was constantly pushing back on new policies and procedures with what-if scenarios. "What if someone doesn't want to be on camera?" "What if someone had already planned to take the day off on the day of our team meeting?" or "What if we already have a good meeting cadence with our customers (are we still obligated to follow the new guidance we've been provided)?"

Those were just a few of the questions I asked—reasonable ones, meant to spark reflection and maybe a little flexibility. Yet instead of being met with gratitude, I was being penalized simply for having the courage to ask them in the first place.

Please don't let haters deter you from finding your voice and using it as you see fit. If this idea is new to you, practice using your voice in less threatening contexts so you build the muscle. Then, as you find your footing, don't be afraid to use your voice to advocate for yourself and others. Here are some ways to ease into speaking up at work.

- An example of a low-stakes scenario might be asking a colleague to copy you on an email to a customer. "Can you please CC me on that note so I can follow up with the customer later?" Start with a courteous ask that provides context and clarity for the other person.
- An example of a medium-stakes scenario might be asking to be invited to a customer call or meeting. "Please go ahead and add me to the invite list so I can hear their objection to the proposal firsthand." Notice how I shifted from a request "can you" to a directive. It's not a question but more of a clear instruction: "Please go ahead and do this."
- An example of a high-stakes scenario could be telling your manager that you disagree with how a customer deal is being handled and suggesting a better approach. For instance, you might say, "I don't know if we're looking at this the right way. If we have them sign a five-year contract to compensate for the service they want to remove from their current agreement, we'll lock in higher revenue." In this last stage, we've moved beyond directives. We're now owning the mic and making a compelling case for our point of view.

I hope this helps you see how taking small steps can build your confidence and strengthen your skills over time. Not everyone will agree with you in every instance, but the more you practice, the better you'll become at handling objections and overcoming roadblocks.

Taking up space is another way to step into your power. This is kind of like what I did in those steering committee meetings. I stopped shrinking myself or trying to make myself likeable to everyone in the room. I just showed up like everyone else did. I deserved to be in the room too and I acted like it. I didn't wait to be asked a question or called on; I just spoke up when I had something to say. I contributed to the conversation, asked questions, and suggested ways we could do whatever we were doing better. I disagreed if I needed to, even with a person more senior than me. I'm not proposing you disregard all cultural and company norms. You should be familiar with how your organization operates and still be willing to push the envelope as you see fit. People will respect you for daring to be bold and brave.

If that sounds daunting, and I can completely understand why it might, try some of these strategies:

- Know your shit. Period. You heard me. You can't walk into a meeting all laissez-faire. You gotta walk into the room prepared, confident, and ready to go. Know the answers to questions you might be asked and come armed with your own questions to drive the conversation.
- Build rapport with your colleagues outside of formal settings so they feel more approachable when the stakes are higher. Invite them to coffee or lunch. Let them get to know you and your working style. This will help them support you more effectively when, or if, the time comes.
- Know who's in the room and pay attention to how people are interacting so you can identify where there might be an opportunity to push back if you feel strongly about an issue. The last thing you want to do is piss off the wrong person or catch someone on a bad day.

Last note I will make around stepping into your power is to encourage you to unleash your awesome. So many of us hide our awesome to make others feel better about themselves. We don't want to threaten or outshine others because it may make them look bad and if others feel bad about themselves, we feel we're being unkind. I call bullshit on all of this.

A perfect example of this is when a colleague and I were both going for promotions. For a while, it felt like we were competing for the same spot. But in reality, that wasn't the case. The company could promote both of us, one of us, or neither of us based entirely on our individual performance.

Once we realized that, we stopped worrying about one-upping each other and focused on doing great work with our own book of business. We even shared best practices to give ourselves the best possible shot.

And guess what? We *both* got promoted.

Remember what I said in an earlier chapter about abundance. Me shining my light has nothing to do with you or your light. You can shine your light too. We can both shine. And we can both be awesome. And what's better than working alongside other awesome people, collaborating on incredible projects, and delivering meaningful outcomes together? Don't believe that there's not enough room or space for all of us to shine. There is. So go ahead. Shine your light boldly and unapologetically!

Be bold and brave

When my manager referred to me as "disruptive," I was offended because I knew he didn't mean it in a nice way. Come to find out that being a "disruptor" is something freaking awesome. According to Arnie Bellini, Managing Partner at Bellini Capital, a disruptor is "someone who isn't afraid to make waves, someone who is constantly pushing the envelope to do things better, without worrying about how things have always been done."[11]

Now tell me again how being a disruptor is a bad thing? I'll wait.

Another name I've been called over the course of stepping into my power is a "truth-teller."[12] A truth-teller is someone who tells the truth, especially about what is *really* happening in a situation. Imagine being the person who says "nah" on a regular basis. Who rejects the gaslighting and performative explanations and instead is honest about what is really occurring. Imagine the power and courage that person has. Imagine the fear someone like that instills in others who know that she will speak truth to power in a heartbeat. Be that person. The world needs you.

I've said this next thing throughout this book, but I will say it again here because it's so important. All this power you reclaim and step into, use it not only for your benefit but for the benefit of others. Be the person who not only advocates for yourself and the things you want but be aware of how you can use your privilege and influence to help lift others or improve their situations.

It doesn't even have to be people you know or agree with. I am part of a women's collective, and I strive to make sure we are inclusive in all that we do. On one occasion, we were planning a talk that I felt would potentially isolate folks I didn't agree with. But that didn't stop me from making sure that the space we created was a safe and brave one for EVERYONE. Even people I didn't know, like, or see eye to eye with. Imagine wielding that kind of power. While most people strive to create a safe space for themselves, real leaders find ways to

---

[11]Link to definition of disruptor: https://www.linkedin.com/pulse/what-does-mean-disrupter-arnie-bellini/
[12]Link to definition of truth-teller: https://dictionary.cambridge.org/us/dictionary/english/truth-teller

create safe spaces for all. Now, that's power being used for the greater good. And that shit is amazing.

Don't shrink or dim your light

Mija, I don't want you to ever be in a situation where you are apologizing for who you are, what you believe, or what you think is right. Those days are gone!

We often shrink or dim our light to make other people feel comfortable. I hope by now I have convinced you that a true jefa is not about that life. We don't exist for the comfort of others, and we don't shrink to appease the needs of others.

We show up fully, completely, imperfectly, and courageously. We take up space, we use our voice, we inspire others, we are healthy, we are joy filled, we believe in ourselves, we embrace our identities, we love our bodies, we trust ourselves, we are not too much, we are more than enough, we know when it's time to cut our losses, we don't need the approval of others, we set and respect boundaries, we love our families (given or chosen), we pour into others while learning from them, we build community, we show up for other people, we ask for help, and we are resilient as fuck.

And another thing. We will step into our magic fully, whenever we choose, in every scenario, to the extent we deem necessary, in ways we know will create impact, for whoever we decide deserves it. And we will do so without asking for permission or seeking approval.

Don't get it twisted. We are perfect just as we are. Even when the world doesn't always deserve us, we show up. We are called to lead, create, become, gather, comfort, serve, and love. And so, we do.

It won't always be easy to be the person you're becoming.

There will be haters. There will be others who try to steal our joy or try to throw us off-kilter. It will take work because we need to be very self-aware, thoughtful, intentional, kind, generous, and more. But it will be worth every ounce of effort we put into creating the life we want and deserve. As the saying goes, nothing good comes easy.[13] We will have to recommit to being our best self every day. We will have to remain positive and steadfast. We will have to recognize that everything we are comes from deep within us. We will have to be brave and bold. We will have to be loud and proud of who we are, where we came from, and what we want for our life and our future. We will pay attention to what is happening around us while remaining clear on our purpose and why.

En resumen

Push through any discomfort you are feeling. Being amazing is hard work but you have more than enough magic in you to be awesome. Claim your space and make your voice heard. On the other side of fear lies FREEDOM. Freedom to show up authentically, to live your life according to your values, to align your work with your purpose, and to take calculated risks based on what you want out of life. But you gotta do the work. Only you hold the key to unlocking the perfect life for you. Are you brave enough to go for it?

Chew on that and these other reflection questions before moving on to the next chapter:

---

[13]The phrase "Nothing good comes easy" reflects the idea that achieving something valuable, meaningful, or worthwhile often requires effort, perseverance, and sometimes sacrifice. The underlying message is that the effort you put in makes the achievement more rewarding.

1. When do you feel most tempted to dim your light or shrink in the presence of others?

   _____

   _____

   _____

   _____

2. When was the last time you spoke up for yourself or others in a way that felt bold and empowering?

   _____

   _____

   _____

   _____

3. How would your life change if you fully embraced your narrative, without fear or hesitation?

   _____

   _____

   _____

   _____

4. How can you push through discomfort to unlock new levels of freedom and success?

_____

_____

_____

_____

CHAPTER 8

NADIE IS COMING TO SAVE YOU

"Querer es poder."[14]

---

[14] This refrán loosely translates to "Wanting is doing," or to say it in a way you might have heard it before, "Where there's a will, there's a way." This saying emphasizes the power of determination and willpower in overcoming challenges and achieving goals. Perseverance is the key message of this refrán.

There are times in your life that make you wonder, is this shit really happening to me? And more importantly, why? Why does it feel like I'm getting overlooked, dismissed, or ignored? Why does it feel like no one sees me or cares that I'm going through it? Why does it feel like even my friends have abandoned me or are sick of hearing me complain? That shit can feel lonely, sad, and extremely isolating.

I've gone through these types of career slumps several times over the years. It feels like things are going from bad to worse or as my mother used to say, "De Guatemala a Guatepeor."[15] What you really need during that time is a friend or colleague who sees you and can relate to the frustration or disappointment you're experiencing. But as I've often said in this book already, most people are focused on their own thing, their own drama, and their own hardships.

---

[15]This refrán loosely translates to "From Guate-bad to Guate-worse." It's a play on words. Guatemala is the name of a country but "mala" by itself means bad. To say something is "Guatepeor" means it went from bad to worse. It humorously describes a situation where someone leaves a bad circumstance only to end up in an even worse one.

I remember going through a particularly rough patch while working for this one manager. It was a weird situation because it was a new team that was forming, and he had specifically invited me to join him on that team. So as far as I could tell, he liked me and valued my contributions. But once we came together as the "new team," it felt like the priorities had changed and the thing that I was most known for was no longer a top priority. That meant I was often left out of customer meetings, product roadmap discussions, etc. Although I had the same knowledge as when I first joined the team, it felt like my value to the group had significantly diminished. I felt very isolated and alone. And I felt like that for several months.

Around the same time, I decided to get involved with some extracurricular activities. I ended up joining a mentoring program through the women's ERG and was matched with a female leader in another part of the organization. This leader was very kind and even though we only met with each other monthly, she listened to my concerns and made me feel heard. "It's not you," my mentor would say. "This guy sounds like he's not a great manager. Stick with it. You are going through a rough patch, and you will come out the other side."

Through the same program, I met another senior leader. He was not my mentor, but he was a mentor to someone else in the program. This leader was great. His eyes would light up every time we would bump into each other. "What are you up to?" this leader would ask. "I know you must be doing great things!" It was weird that he thought so highly of me and expected "great things from me." He barely knew me, but he was so encouraging and kind. He somehow saw that I was going through a hard time, and I don't know why, he decided he would offer the words of encouragement that I so desperately needed to hear. To this day, I'm still not sure why he took such an interest in me. All I can say is that I'm ever so grateful he did. He was like an angel sent down to carry me through a time in my journey when I felt alone, scared, and helpless.

And while his support came when I needed it the most, it didn't do much to change my work situation. My manager still ignored me. He still didn't find a way to tap into my talents and skills. At the same time, business conditions were unstable, and one of the sales team members was eventually let go.

It was the letting go of that person that changed everything for me although I didn't realize it at the time. It was decided that I would temporarily step into this sales role since I was currently underutilized, and we now had this open position. I had never done sales in my entire life and was somewhat opposed to doing it since my general impression of salespeople was not good. Nevertheless, it was a situation of "Esto es lo que hay,"[16] and so I stepped into the role with the intention of doing my best.

A few weeks later, I was out on my own visiting with customers and prospects. Just a few weeks after that, I was closing my first few deals and showing some real promise in the role. I don't remember when, or if, we ever discussed it, but I ended up being a permanent part of that sales team. Over time, I expanded my role to support the entire non-US region, while keeping clients in Miami and Puerto Rico.

I had gone from zero to one hundred in just a matter of months. My career really took off. I was leaning into this role with everything I had. Opportunity had come knocking and I fully embraced my new circumstances. I was in that role for several years. It was a role that allowed me to travel to many places, establish myself as an

---

[16]This cultural expression loosely translates to "This is what there is" or similar to what you might have heard before "It is what it is." It's often used in informal contexts to convey that a situation is not ideal, but it's the only option available.

exemplary customer-facing professional, and learn a lot about myself in the process.

In the end, the support I received helped but it was my grit and resilience that took me to the next level. Community and support are needed and important. However, we are the only ones that can change our path forward. We are the only ones that can really step up when opportunities are presented. We are the only ones that can decide that we want to succeed and then figure out a way how.

Amiga, you are the author of your story and the architect of your life. No one else has the power and influence you have to change things for the better. Sometimes we get lucky and have an opportunity present itself. What comes next is a result of what we decide to do with whatever breaks we are presented with.

Know what you want

When you know what you want, it will be easier to seize opportunities when they arise. You should know what your goals are. Both personally and professionally. Ideally, these goals should be based on your values and purpose. When there is misalignment, it causes all kinds of problems.

If my goal is to help people, especially those who are overlooked or underestimated, then working at a bank might not be aligned with my goals and purpose. I use the word "might" because it's not all black and white.

I remember working at a financial institution, constantly struggling to align my values with the role. While it wasn't a perfect fit, it was manageable. Doable. Until I could find something that made more sense for me. I wasn't ready for a big change just yet. But I would be soon enough.

During this waiting period, I invested a lot of time getting more familiar with my purpose and my nonnegotiables (where I draw the line). I journaled, took time to reflect on what I wanted for my future, and read books that challenged my tendency to not rock the boat.

The result of this intentionality was clarity, courage, and readiness for what came next. I knew I had marketable skills, and with greater clarity about what I wanted, I could pursue jobs that aligned with my goals and ambition.

I'm telling you this to remind you that you have choices, no matter the situation. This life is yours to live. Be mindful of making personal and professional decisions that are rooted in what you want out of your life and journey and not what others expect of you.

I speak from experience because I spent a lot of my life people-pleasing in one way or another. The only way out of that cycle is realizing that *you* are responsible for your own happiness. And that means making decisions that serve you. Yes, it might feel like you're disappointing others. And yes, that can be uncomfortable. But you have to move through that discomfort to create the life you want and deserve.

I'm not sure if it's a Latina thing to want your mother's approval or if that is a universal thing every young person experiences. But more than anything, I wanted my mother to be proud of me and the life choices I was making. And while she was in fact proud of me, I was deeply unhappy.

So, little by little, I found ways to become happier. Sometimes it meant finding a company whose mission aligned with my values. Other times, it was about setting boundaries to make space for things

I loved and that gave me purpose outside of work. And on other occasions, it was about working for a company that allowed me to engage in meaningful projects and initiatives as part of my job. My passion and commitment to ERG work grew during this period of my journey.

My point here is that I don't want you to hold yourself back because you're trying to people please or live by other people's ideas of what is expected of you. Fuck that. Live your life on your terms based on what matters to you. And dream big as you do this. The more you are aligned with your life's work, the bigger the dreams.

Show up for yourself

Showing up for yourself means making your aspirations known. This is how you set yourself up for success. It means having an honest conversation with your manager, mentor, or senior leader and letting them know where you see yourself in a few years.

Don't be afraid to ask for their help in getting to where you want to go. Even if your dream seems too big. Yes, I've had managers tell me, "It's not realistic to expect (fill in the blank)." That did not deter me, and I am here to tell you, don't let it deter you either. Maybe a "fast promotion" is not something that happens every day, but if I'm doing the work, can you help me to make it happen?

Sometimes I could see the sad look in their eyes as I enthusiastically talked about my aspirations and goals.

They didn't think I would succeed.

Maybe because I am a woman, maybe because I am Latina, or maybe because they just didn't think I was talented enough to achieve the things I hoped for. Who knows? I still had the audacity to dream big and share those dreams with others. And that alone, takes courage.

And as I repeated my dreams and goals out loud, I would sometimes notice a shift in the ways I was treated or talked to. On many occasions, I broke through and got others to see for me, what I saw for myself.

Advocate for yourself publicly and privately. Share your dreams out loud. Tell folks what you're hoping for. It will scare some people. Others might feel threatened. All that is on them. You're telling others what you want because it opens the door for other people to share in the responsibility of bringing it to life. When people realize you are serious about your hopes and dreams, they will be drawn to help make it happen.

Make bold moves

Move with intention. Don't be afraid to make bold moves as you go after what you want and deserve. In those moments when I felt isolated and alone in my job, I was not clear about what would give me purpose.

But once I was clear that the sales role was a great opportunity, I was bold and audacious.

I went after prospects in ways that got me closed contracts at my first customer meetings. I would pay very close attention in customer conversations and uncover additional needs that I could help fill. More than half my book was made up of customers that purchased more than one product.

I could sniff out business development opportunities because I got that good.

Don't settle for less than you deserve. I'm so glad things worked out the way they did for me. I was brought over to the team to meet one need, and I ended up using a whole different set of skills to bring more value to the organization. I had the skills and the experience and truly deserved the opportunity I got. And I didn't pooh-pooh it. I saw the opportunity for what it was and used it as a stepping stone to even bigger and better roles.

I didn't always get along with my ex-mother-in-law but one thing she said that stuck with me was "If you don't ask, you don't get." Said differently, "Hungry mouths get fed." When you are clear on your purpose, when you are aligned with your values, when you are showing up for yourself, then it's a lot easier for you to ask for what you need. Whether it's a promotion, a raise, a big client, a special assignment, go for it.

I remember when I was working with a lot of customers in Latin America, I got my manager to pay for business Spanish classes. I already spoke Spanish at home but there were a lot of business terms and phrases that I struggled with. To do my job better, it made sense for the company to sponsor this type of professional development. So, I asked for them to sponsor this training and they did. I also joined a Portuguese course my colleagues were taking in a different part of the bank. I took a sales course that taught me how to close more deals. Then, I used our company's customer relationship management system to track all my interactions and measure my progress. Once I got clear on the direction I was moving in, I could ask for a whole lot of things. And most of the things I asked for, I got.

En resumen

Be clear on where you see yourself going in the long- and short-term. Know what baby steps will likely get you there and start working on those. Always be ready for when the next opportunity presents itself.

Advocate for yourself so that the opportunity is even a possibility. Ask for help, share your dreams, be audacious, and set bold goals.

To save yourself, you must be willing to take risks to get the outcomes you want. I've had to step into roles for which I had no experience, leave a company and go somewhere completely new, and trust people who said they wanted to help me. I had no guarantee that any of these gambles would work out. I had to see the bigger picture that would help move me closer to the outcomes I was hoping for.

My last piece of advice in this chapter is to not feel guilty or apologetic for wanting more for yourself, your family, and community. Remember, the "more" you seek is defined by you. My more was feeling more purposeful. Your more could be making more money, saving more toward your retirement and children's education, maybe even buying your parents a house.

When you realize no one but you is coming to save you, achieving your dreams becomes all the more satisfying and rewarding. I hope this reminder inspires you to stay steadfast on the path toward your goals.

And now, here are some reflection questions as we close out this chapter:

1. In what areas of your life are you still waiting for someone to "save" you?

   _____

   _____

   _____

   _____

2. What is one big dream you've put on hold and why?

3. When was the last time you advocated for yourself?

4. What risks have you taken that led to positive outcomes?

CHAPTER 9

BE YOU SIN EXCUSAS

"Crea fama y acuéstate a dormir."[17]

---

[17]This refrán loosely translates to "Create fame and go to sleep" or said in a way that makes more sense "Create a reputation and then you can rest." It suggests that once you've established a certain perception of yourself, that reputation will precede you, influencing how others view and treat you. It can be used both positively and negatively. Recognizing the lasting impact of our actions and behaviors is the key message of this refrán.

"I identify as a Latina and a Woman of Color." That's mostly how I introduce myself these days. And it's wild to me. That I would offer that intimate window into something so personal to perfect strangers. When I think back to the early days in my career journey, I would never have offered up that detail about myself. It was too much information. But more importantly, it was unsafe to do so as my Latinidad and underrepresented status could be used against me.

This isn't hyperbole. I'm just keeping it real. Ask any Latina or Woman of Color how they feel when their identity comes up at work. I think some words you might get back include worried, anxious, and concerned. Especially women of my generation. Back in the nineties, it was a scary time to come out as an "underrepresented employee." They didn't call us DEI (Diversity, Equity, and Inclusion) hires back then. They just assumed we were hired because of affirmative action. And it was perfectly OK to be othered. I know firsthand.

I have receipts.

There was the one time I showed up early to a team breakfast meeting and had the senior leader ask if I had a knife handy because

"Don't Hispanic people always carry a knife?" Mind you this was an SVP of a large bank who felt he could say that, to my face, in a public setting, as "a joke." I didn't know what a microaggression was back then. Not even sure if the word existed. But I felt like I had been sucker punched without any warning. I sat uncomfortably at the meeting until the end when I pulled my manager aside and told him what happened. He was a white man too but still managed to understand how devastating the comment came across to me.

Then there were the times when I would share my full first name, Hadyla, and immediately get asked, "What kind of name is that?" which led to a whole conversation about how it's an Arabic name even though, I myself, don't have Arab roots. Sometimes, before I "came out" as Latina, people would think I was Middle Eastern because they were quick to put me in a box, even if it was the wrong one.

And then there was the time when, despite graduating college with a 3.98 GPA, I sat in an interview and was asked why my SAT scores were so low. I was being questioned about a test I had taken four years earlier, despite my highly successful college career. It made me question my abilities. And it was humiliating. Also, it really pissed me off. It took everything in me to calmly explain how standardized tests unfairly disadvantage communities of color. A fun fact I had picked up along my journey and one that I wish he had too. I got that job. And spent many years working alongside folks like him. It was the fact that he put me in the hot seat unnecessarily that still bothers me.

These days I don't play. I put it out there that I'm Latina and a Woman of Color. That's something you're going to want to know about me because it drives everything that I do and all the ways I show up.

Let's start with my LinkedIn profile and Latina-owned business. The first thing you will see right below my name on my profile is

"Empowering Latinas & Women of Color." That's my job. That's my purpose. That's why I'm here. That's why I'm writing this book. When I think about my WHY and my PURPOSE, I founded Boldly Speaking to share my journey, insights, and lessons learned, all in the hope of empowering Latinas and other Women of Color to rise and thrive in the corporate world or in whatever path they choose.

I devote a lot of my time to working with Latinas and Women of Color. In 2024, I launched a LinkedIn Live show called *Latinas: Front & Center*. Why? Because Latinas are too often left out of conversations. Our contributions are often ignored and dismissed. Many people believe we should be grateful for whatever is given to us and try to make us feel bad when we expect or want more. We are rarely considered subject matter experts or leaders in our fields. We don't always receive recognition, public praise, or acknowledgment from our peers for our achievements. Nor do we get invited to important discussions that drive key decisions. That's why I've taken it upon myself to celebrate Latinas doing amazing things. And to showcase the great things we're doing with the world.

I'm also a member of a few Latinx serving organizations. My favorite one, hands down, is Lean In Latinas. This is an organization where I felt welcome on day one, have found sisters-in-the-work, and where my contributions are celebrated and amplified. It is through this amazing organization that I have the opportunity, through our collective efforts, to offer more of the same to other Latinas. I have volunteered a lot of my time with this organization because their mission and values are firmly aligned with my own.

It's not as scary to come out as Latina these days.

It's truly our time to show up, show out, be authentic, and unapologetically embrace all that we are, want, and bring to the table. We are who we've been waiting for, and it's our time to shine!

Know who you are

I don't want to sound like a broken record but it's crucial for you to know what you stand for. You must know your values and make decisions that align with them. Your values should guide the direction you move in and shape where you want to go. Sometimes being clear on what you stand for means unlearning harmful thoughts and beliefs. Other times, your values will lead you to adapt mindsets that offer you more opportunity. Trusting yourself as you navigate your path is key. Because when you know who you are, you will know what things to say YES to and conversely where to draw the line on unhealthy habits and people.

Please don't compromise your values out of uncertainty and fear. I've done this. And I will say that 99.9 percent of the time, I knew that I was compromising my values even as I was taking the step forward. Be aware of red flags and listen to the warning signals that will tell you to proceed with caution. In my life, I've had to walk away from friendships, marriages, jobs, and business arrangements that did not align with my values. I even had to walk away from not one, but two, churches whose values did not align with my own.

To be able to walk away from two churches requires a shit ton of self-awareness. The process I follow usually starts with my body telling me something isn't right. But I need my brain to explain to me why before I take any action. For me, it's crucial to understand why the thing isn't working or no longer suits me. I want to be clear around WHY I'm moving away from something so that I know WHAT I want to move toward. This process helps me to move toward something that will be better for me and not just away from something that isn't working.

All of this is going to feel super uncomfortable the first time you do it. And potentially every time you make a decision that aligns with who you are and what you stand for. Walking away from a marriage is not easy. Quitting a job may leave you in financial distress. Changing your mind after having said YES to something may make you feel like a failure.

Be strategic with your decisions, and know that sooner or later, you'll have to face that feeling in your stomach (or whatever signals to you that something's out of alignment). Sometimes, I can fix the situation right away. Sometimes it takes months or years for me to make a move that will put me on the right path.

Fear is a hell of a drug, and it will keep you frozen in place for as long as you let it.

Whenever friends ask me about my divorce process, I explain it this way. First, you must be aware that you are unhappy in your marriage. But that's only half of the process. Next, you must be willing to do something about it. Some people stay stuck in that first part and never move out of the awareness phase. Awareness without action is not going to do much to change your situation. There must come a point where you say ENOUGH. This is not what I want for me and I'm willing to do whatever it takes to find joy and peace again.

The same is true for any other decision you make that isn't working for you. You must be aware that the situation is not working AND you must be willing to take whatever actions are necessary to make the situation better. Avoid using discomfort and fear as excuses for remaining stuck in a cycle that doesn't work for you.

Show up fully

Girl, don't let anyone dim your light. Let me say that again. Do not allow others to make you feel small, want to shrink, or dull your shine.

You are magic.
You are energy.
You are light.
You are fire.
You are joy.
You are hope.

I don't think enough people tell us this and so it makes it hard for us to believe it and own it. I've had managers call me loud, disruptive, and pushy. Yes, I am those things. I'm also incredibly curious, a thoughtful listener, and a high performer.

None of us are just one thing. We are perfectly imperfect and that's just fine. My hope is that you will be way more aware of the things that set you apart and be willing to lean into your strengths.

One such strength is your Latinidad. Sometimes embracing your Latinidad means laughing louder than everyone else, rocking your hoops, wearing bold lip colors, or asking for more plantain chips in the break room. But mostly it just means that we celebrate who we are. That we have pride in our ancestors and cultural roots. That we use refránes freely and translate them for our colleagues and friends. That we embrace a particular cultural nuance and not apologize for it. That we come out of the proverbial shadows and instead step into the light. That we reclaim the beauty of what sets us apart and lead with cultura.

This book has been all about my transformation. And I want it to be about yours too. In my case, there came a time where I could remain silent no more. That calladita mindset was not for me. In fact, I ultimately found the whole notion of remaining silent and doing nothing as I watched situations play out to be quite triggering. I felt stifled, resentful, and maybe even a little bitter. I saw the ways my colleagues spoke up bravely and confidently even when they did not have experience or facts to back up their positions. And I noticed how I would get treated or talked to if I asked a question or low-key challenged an assumption that was made by a senior leader or colleague.

And so, I made a promise to myself. I would remain calladita no more. I would instead walk into rooms like I belonged there. Even when people tried to make me feel otherwise. I spoke up not only on behalf of myself but for others too. I dared to speak truth to power in moments that mattered even if it meant that other people would try to silence me or deny their role in certain outcomes. I made it a point to bring others with me. To remind other women I met about what I saw in them and how they too should be showing up in bigger ways. I set out to find other women that shared my values, my purpose, and my vision. I built communities and programs with these women often in exchange for nothing but their friendship and sisterhood. I developed a point of view. I wrote more. I put myself out there. I stepped into more leadership roles. I took more risks. I made bold choices and decisions. I cut some people out of my life. And created space for new co-conspirators.

The more space I occupied, the more powerful I felt. And the more powerful I felt, the more inclined I was to use my power and privilege to advocate for myself and others. It was a powerful cycle of the highest magnitude. Some people were excited to see me enter a room. Others shifted uncomfortably in their seats. All good signs in my book.

Make others acknowledge your presence

That I even have to write about this topic is telling enough. Why would someone's presence go unacknowledged? My guess is that there are all sorts of reasons. Mostly having to do with power. People ignore or dismiss you to make themselves feel bigger and more powerful. Or they want you to know you are not welcome in a space. Or that they don't care what you think and are not looking for your input. Or that they don't believe you deserve a seat at a given table. Blah, blah, blah.

My take is that people like us belong in every room and at all the tables. We have unique perspectives to bring to conversations and, when we don't speak up, the places where we work are missing out.

One strategy I've used to get others to acknowledge me is to specifically greet them when I come into the room. "Good morning, Joe" and wait for their response. As ridiculous as it sounds, I can think of some people who didn't appreciate me doing this. Can you imagine?

I've also come prepared with questions and well-thought-out suggestions for the problems we were trying to solve. You can't deny preparedness and excellence.

Well, technically you could. Have I stated an idea, had it ignored, and then seen the room respond positively when another colleague brought up the same suggestion? Yes. Have I also had allies in the room who acknowledged it was my idea first? Also, yes.

Regardless of the dynamics at play, being prepared and ready to share your perspective is key to making your presence felt. Don't half step it. Be intentional about the outcomes you want from a meeting or call. And don't let office politics or folks who try to undermine you stand in your way.

Listen, if you are like me, you've seen and heard it all. People will treat you one way outside of the room, and a completely different way inside the room. Some of that is posturing. Also, let's face it. We work with a lot of brownnosers who are just looking out for themselves.

None of this really matters in the end. Because when we enter a room and are looking to make an impact, we are relying on our own skills and talent first and foremost. The support from colleagues and friends is nice to have but not necessary because we won't always have it. We can't rely on others to make us feel seen. We must be able to enter spaces and stand on our own two feet.

If I'm honest, it's when I have felt alone in a room that I have wanted to shrink and settle into the background of a meeting or discussion the most. But over time, I learned to lean in, step into the conversation, and have fun. I almost always bring a different perspective to the conversation and so really, this is our time to shine. I have gotten more comfortable with this. And yet, there are still times when I enter a room to silence. And in those moments, I will either greet the people I know or start walking around the room and introducing myself to the people I've never met.

You belong. I belong. We belong. And the best thing we can do is to act like it.

Be audacious as you walk through the world

When we are on fire, the people around us will know it. And they will often clear the path or get out of our way. And so that is why I want to encourage you to move through life fearlessly. Don't be afraid of the power and influence you hold. Step into that shit. Be bold and brave. Take more chances. Shoot your damn shot. We can't have all this power and freedom and keep it under lock and key. It's our responsibility to unleash our awesome into the world as we see fit. To enter a space, elevate it, and ensure we leave it better than we found it. To find new and different ways to spread our light and love.

And, amiga, walk with conviction as you slay. You heard me. Stand tall. Shoulders back. Head held high. Notice your surroundings. Be present and confident as you engage with others. Move with purpose. Make every space come alive with your energy. Set the tone with your presence. Elevate the vibe wherever you go. Have a sense of urgency without rushing through conversations and encounters. Reflect confidence and control because, girl, you got this. And everyone knows it.

Say less. Literally. Let your actions do the talking. Are you as sick as I am of people who talk a good game and have nothing to show for it? Yeah, me too. We are not those kinds of people. We are women of impact, of change, of transformation, of courage. We leave everything better than we found it. We don't play. We come to win. We are here to get shit done and take names. We are here for ourselves, for the community, and for the next generation. We are here to claim our power, our pay, and our place. We are not backing down, shying away, or sugarcoating our messages. We are here to work, to get our flowers, and to move on to places where we are needed next. So, say less and do more.

En resumen

When you know who you are, you're in a position of power. Self-awareness is a skill that is highly underrated. Not enough people talk about the things you can do and the heights you can reach when you know yourself and you step into who that is fully and unapologetically.

Self-awareness starts with knowing your values and purpose. Everything else comes from that place. So do the work, lean in, and enjoy the ride. Leverage the power and influence you have and own every situation. Don't be afraid to wield your power to make things happen. Be fearless. Move with confidence. Even in situations that are new to you or that seem scary or uncertain. When you make moves from a solid foundation, you're setting yourself up to be exactly where you need to be. Trust yourself and what you know. It will lead you to places you've never dreamed of. Imagine that.

Before we move on to the next chapter on remaining steadfast and positive, here are some questions for you to reflect on:

1. Have you ever compromised your true self out of fear of judgment or rejection?

   _____

   _____

   _____

2. In what situations do you tend to dim your light?

   _____

   _____

   _____

3. When have you experienced knowing and owning who you are so deeply that it empowered you in a difficult situation?

   _____

   _____

   _____

   _____

4. What would it look like for you to live fearlessly?

   _____

   _____

   _____

   _____

CHAPTER 10

STEADFAST Y POSITIVA

"Lo que está pa' ti, nadie te lo quita."[18]

---

[18]This refrán loosely translates to "What is meant for you will not be taken from you," or said in a way that might be more familiar to you, "What is meant for you will not pass you by." It suggests that there are things in life that are meant only for us. And that instead of despairing, we should remain ready to receive them. Trusting in the timing of life is the key message of this refrán.

Would I ever make good money again, be able to travel, save for my future, and not be so financially stressed out? This is the question I found myself asking after I came back from volunteering overseas and before I found a job in tech.

This was an extremely stressful time for me. I was working for a nonprofit and was making half the salary I was earning before I went on mission. I didn't expect to make the same salary after leaving corporate, but my current path was not sustainable. About half of my take-home pay was going toward the rent. The rest was going toward medical bills and food. I had no money to shop for new clothes or for self-care treats like massages. I stopped meeting up with friends and family for brunch or dinner because I simply did not have the money. It was a tough season for me. I felt lonely, super stressed, and emotionally drained.

When I got back from living in Bolivia, I was dealing with a lot of health issues. I didn't know it at the time, but I was going through menopause. My hair was falling out. I was getting awful hot flashes. And I was putting on weight even though I was keeping my same diet and exercise routine. It got to the point where I no longer recognized my body. Not in a physical sense. I still looked more or less the same. I'm talking about the ways I felt helpless in trying to feel better. I knew I had to make some changes.

The other "souvenir" I brought back from Bolivia was a sensitive gut. I mean everything I ate gave me a stomachache. Sometimes for days or weeks at a time. I was going for all kinds of tests with my regular doctor, but I wasn't seeing a lot of progress. I decided to hit up a naturopathic doctor that specialized in stomach issues, hair loss, and other symptoms I was experiencing. It was expensive but I needed to get better and feel like my old self again, so I prioritized this expense.

It was around this time that I started eating gluten-free. It was not an easy transition for me. I'm a New Yorker. We eat bagels for breakfast, pizza for lunch, and pasta for dinner. And all of these foods were my favorite things to eat. It was such a low point in my life. To have to give up these things I knew and loved for the rest of my life was a big loss. I don't think the people around me appreciated the grief and sadness I experienced during this time.

WHY ME? Why this? Why now?

Haha, I sound so dramática. The truth is it was a very hard time for me, and I can feel the sadness even as I think back to that time. I'm better now. I've found my gluten-free-friendly spots and I'm perfectly OK with eating brown rice pasta and oat flour pancakes.

But I give you this context because I want you to know everything I was experiencing at that time: financial stress, health issues, sadness, anxiety, loneliness, exhaustion, and grief. It was a time that sucked for me in monumental proportions. And so, I decided to add to all of that, a job search.

To say the search didn't go well is an understatement. People acted like those twenty years of corporate experience I had didn't matter. Hello, are you fucking kidding me? I worked for big companies too: Accenture, JPMorgan Chase, BNY Mellon. The companies and organizations I met with were unimpressed and not willing to give me a chance to get back into corporate after having been gone for just a few short years.

I learned so many lessons during this time. People can be cruel. People can be unkind. People can be reckless with their decisions, having no idea the impact their choices have on the lives of others. One of the lowest points of this period was when I interviewed with a previous employer for a job I held just years before and was told I was not qualified for the role. Ha! That was such a slap in the face.

I decided to up my game because I was serious about making more money, getting access to better health insurance, and saving for my future. That was my carrot, and I had my eyes on the prize. I hired a coach. This person helped me redo my resume and cover letter. They also helped me as I prepped for interviews. They coached me as I wrote my thank you letters and follow-up notes. We were a team with one goal in mind. And after two long years of searching, I finally found a job that had me back in the six-figure game, offered 100 percent medical coverage, and allowed me to save toward my future again.

I did it. I didn't do it alone. It didn't happen overnight. I didn't make as much as I was making before I went overseas but I was back in the game. I was back where I needed to be and would soon work my way back to where I rightfully belonged. There was light at the end of the tunnel.

There's a saying in Spanish that my friend likes to say: "No te puedes tirar a morir." Loosely translated it means, "You can't give up and die," or simply put, "You can't give up during difficult times." And shit, I feel that refrán because it's so damn true. There will be ups and downs in life, but we must remain resilient and trust that what is meant for us will not pass us by.

If I'm honest, most of the time giving up is not even an option. I always find a way to dust myself off and keep going. And so should you.

What is meant for you will find you

I'm wondering how many of you reading this book really believe this. I know I do, and it is one of the most comforting things in the world to know that what is meant for you will not pass you by. Everything in the Universe is aligning in this very moment for it to happen. Shit, if that doesn't make you sleep well at night, what will?

I think an important aspect of making the magic moment happen is to have a lot of clarity. In my case, I knew I wanted a solid paying job that would remove the financial burden I was experiencing at the time. That was my driver. I wanted a job that would set me up for financial success. And I kept looking and securing the support I needed until I found it.

Sometimes we get a NO. I got hundreds of them. NOs can be interpreted in lots of different ways. Not now. Not here. Not with this company. Not in this town. Not ever. Most of the time, I have found the NOs I received to be a blessing in disguise.

There was one job that I didn't get during that time. The company was based in Northern California, and they flew me out for the final interview. I have family in California, so I stayed for the weekend to look at apartments. I was ready to make this opportunity become my new reality. I didn't get that job. And I was devastated. Fast forward to today, that company is now defunct. If I had gone with them, I would have been out of a job, living on the other side of the country, and back where I started.

So not getting that job ended up being a real blessing. I think that happens more than we know and realize. Our job is not necessarily to question why things happen as they do. Instead, I think it's about doing the work and staying ready.

Doing the work is about knowing what you want, preparing for your interviews, researching the best path to get you to the next step, and meeting people who can give you insights, or in some cases, real support to help you meet your goal.

Staying ready is about your mindset. You don't know when what you have been waiting for will come. You just don't. You could be looking for five days or for five years. You could be taking courses, developing content, building thought leadership, surrounding yourself with community for months and then one day, opportunity comes knocking. I like to stay ready for when these opportunities come so I can have the best chance of thriving in my new role, position, appointment, assignment, endeavor, or undertaking.

It all starts with mindset

Let's dive a bit more into mindset because remaining steadfast is absolutely a mind game.

Some techniques that have worked for me include prayer and journaling. But the one that has worked the most is imagining what my life would be like with the thing I desire or, what is widely known as, visual manifestation.

- **Prayer:** I was raised Catholic, so during tough times, I have turned to the Bible to read about those who came before me, their struggles, and how their faith in God led them to

great blessings. Looking for some inspiration? Read the story of Job.
- **Journaling:** There have been times in my life when I journaled daily, especially after a breakup or during tough periods. In those moments, journaling helped me air out my grievances and reflect on what my heart truly desired.
- **Visual manifestation:** This is the thing you see all over the internet when people say they are "manifesting" this or "manifesting" that. It's about vividly picturing the outcomes you want in your mind and really feeling the emotions of that visualization as if it's already happening. Whew! It's powerful stuff and I highly recommend it.[19]

There's enough for all of us

This goes back to the abundance mindset we talked about in the chapter on building community. I can (and should) celebrate the success of others even as I wait for my time to arrive. I won't be triggered when others are getting their moment and having their time in the spotlight. I will be joy filled and celebrate with and for them.

I have so many amazing women in my network right now. I'm talking about powerhouse women who are always reaching for the stars. I've had some of these women on my show *Latinas: Front & Center*. This space is all about amplifying their voices and giving them their flowers in a very public way. I have been in awe of all my guests

---

[19]This works with every aspect of your life. I used to do this ALL. THE. TIME. When I was a teenager, at bedtime, I'd imagine me and my crush talking, walking together, and kissing, then fall asleep with a big fat smile on my face.

because they absolutely embody what it means to go for what you want unapologetically. As I interview guests and celebrate alongside them, I am reminded that part of remaining steadfast and positive is creating space for others to shine. Because today it's their turn. And my time is coming.

Yaaas! My time is coming. And yours is too! We will have many moments to celebrate along our journey. Many milestones to recognize and mark. Promotions. Salary increases. New jobs. New roles. Board member seats. Leadership positions. Certifications received. Business deals closed. Financial goals reached.

Everything is lining up for us as it should, and in the perfect moment, we will be blessed in ways we hoped for and sometimes in ways we didn't think possible. Because God is that good.

Keep going

Until your perfect moment arrives, you can help yourself by remaining steadfast and focused.

Process disappointments. There will be many of them. Failed relationships. Career setbacks. Ghosting. Layoffs. Financial struggles. Betrayal. Loss. Missed opportunities. Bad decisions. Unfulfilled goals.

Really process them. And then let them go. I know so many people who get stuck when life throws them a curveball or an unexpected setback. You can't get stuck, amiga. Feel your feels and move on. Take whatever time you need but don't get stuck. Seek professional help if you need to. It's important to let go of our disappointments and setbacks to create space to receive the good stuff that's coming.

And on that note, I urge you to get back on the proverbial horse as soon as you are able. I honestly feel like I have a gift from my ancestors in this regard. I am super resilient (not perfect) and am often able to get over my setbacks quickly. I process them and I let them go. What does processing look like? For me, I might allow myself a little time to ruminate on the setback and then I move on. Or maybe I'll journal about what happened and then move on. Or I might have a conversation with a comadre or trusted friend about what happened and then I move on. Notice I say I move on. Cause we really have to. We cannot get stuck because it will ruin our vibe, our emotional state, and our essence. We gotta move through it and get to the other side.

If you are having trouble finding your way back to being positive and steadfast, try counting your blessings. Literally. Like open up a new doc or journal page and make a list of the things you are grateful for. Your health. Your friendships. The roof over your head. The food in your fridge. The kindness of a stranger. Money in the bank. You get the idea.

This will bring you back to center and allow you to get excited for what's coming. Because something is coming for you. Something is always brewing, and it will come at the perfect time. Our job is to remain steadfast, clear, focused, and ready to receive it!

En resumen

Be patient, my friend. What you want and hope for is coming. It may not always look like what you thought or expected but it's on its way. Stay ready for the blessings that are coming to you and that may very well represent a new chapter in your life.

You can't rush the Universe. You just can't. Everything will unfold as it needs to. Focus on counting your blessings, processing your disappointments, and keeping a positive mindset. When you do these things, you are creating space for newness, abundance, and receiving. So clear that space up, sis! You want to have plenty of room for all the miracles that will soon be unfolding just for you!

And remember, things won't always go your way. That's to be expected. You have the most power when you dust yourself off and get back in the game. When you remain unrattled and undeterred. You must trust what the Universe is preparing for you. And you can do that best when you are ready to receive.

As I close out this chapter, I'm leaving you with a few questions to reflect on:

1. Recall a time when you faced a setback but believed that what was meant for you would eventually come. What fueled that belief?

   _____

   _____

   _____

   _____

2. Do you do a good job of celebrating the achievement of others while staying focused on your own journey?

   _____

   _____

   _____

   _____

3. When you face disappointments, what motivates you to "get back on the horse"?

   _____

   _____

   _____

   _____

4. What actions are you taking to prepare yourself for the opportunities that are coming your way?

   _____

   _____

   _____

   _____

CHAPTER 11

BRING OTHERS CONTIGO

"Quien siembra con amor, cosecha con abundancia."[20]

---

[20]This refrán loosely translates to "Who sows with love reaps with abundance." When you put love, effort, and positive energy into what you do, whether it's work, relationships, or personal growth, you will see positive, abundant results in return. The quality of your efforts and the mindset you bring to them are the key messages of this refrán.

I've had exactly one manager in my life that I admired and respected and who treated me with kindness and generosity. She is a Woman of Color like me and I trusted her from the moment we met until my last day on her team. She saw my potential and that inspired me to show up as my best self in my role. She spoke my name in rooms where I was not present (in only the best ways) and I would often hear about it from my colleagues and friends. She had my back when others questioned my authority, always redirecting them to me and ensuring my power was mine, not borrowed from her. She coached me behind closed doors about the best ways to achieve the outcomes I was hoping for. She praised me publicly and was quick to give me my flowers in front of her manager and other senior leaders. She sponsored me for promotion, approved continuing education opportunities, and ALWAYS made me feel good about my contributions and hopeful about what was yet to come.

It was from this amazing manager that I learned how to be a good leader. She demonstrated through her deeds that bringing others along is not a one-and-done thing. She saw my raw talent, and for whatever reason, she decided she was going to go all in on me. She was betting on my future, on my talents, and on my ability to ascend into leadership. She didn't just do it one day or one time. She was consistently a sponsor of my work and contributions and others knew it. She was highly respected and extended that social capital to me. She allowed me to make mistakes and yet was quick to point out ways I could be more effective. She pulled me aside when needed and still allowed me to grow and shine. Just when I thought her generosity or kindness had seen its best days, she would surprise me with yet another opportunity or kind gesture. There truly were no limits to her support of me and my dreams. Her belief in my talents got me through many difficult times. I never felt alone or like I could be harmed because she 100 percent had my back.

I wasn't even ten years into my career when I worked for her. There were still a lot of lessons that I would learn and managers that I would work for. It's only looking back that I can see how incredible she was and the impact she had on my career. She taught me a lot about being kind, generous, and supportive. She was a total badass at the company where we worked and yet she was so compassionate and reassuring in my interactions with her.

Having her in my life taught me how to be a generous leader. I learned from her that I lose nothing when I build others up. When I pour into others, it's my cup that gets full. When I focus on giving, I receive so much joy and satisfaction from seeing others grow. When I encourage others to unleash their awesome, there's a part of me that becomes a little more awesome in the process.

Lately I've been saying YES to so much in my life. I have reached a point where pouring into others is very much aligned with my purpose. I'm in a season of giving and it is bringing me peace, joy, and calm. I don't remember exactly when it happened but somewhere along my journey, it stopped being about ME and it started being about US. When one of us wins, we all win. The sign of a great leader is someone who understands that leading the way is a force multiplier that empowers others to unleash their greatness and drives a bigger impact.

I'm not the only one who sees things this way. On my LinkedIn show *Latinas: Front & Center*, I interview Latina leaders from all kinds of industries. I've met with authors, engineers, doctors, marketers, HR professionals, entrepreneurs, sales leaders, and more. Every single one of them, regardless of their age or title, is a leader in the Latinx community because their priority is to give back, pave the way, and otherwise lead with cultura.

Lead with cultura

Let's talk about it. What does leading with cultura mean and what does it look like?

Leading with cultura is about lighting the path for other mujeres and doing so in a way that makes them feel valued and appreciated. If you're like me, you might feel ignored or dismissed in some of the rooms you enter. So do our younger sisters. As a Latina leader, you have to find ways to stop this from happening. Leading with cultura is saying, "I see you and you belong here too."

Other ways I lead with cultura include using refránes to pass down and share cultural knowledge and wisdom with others. I also show up authentically and unapologetically as a first-gen Latina, born in the US to Puerto Rican parents. Sometimes that means being the loudest person in the room (literally and figuratively). Other times it means I use my lived experience to put myself in someone else's shoes and understand their perspective. Still other times it means that I spend extra time with someone who looks like me or whose lived experience reminds me of my own. I will go above and beyond to make sure that person feels included, valued, and encouraged to show up fully and unapologetically.

Leading with cultura also means we show up for each other and want to see each other win. I don't need to have a personal relationship with you to be happy that you're winning and to recognize that when one Latina breaks down a door, many of us get to pass through.

I want to remind you about the abundance mindset I've talked about over and over again in this book. You might be wondering why I talk about it so much. Well, if I'm honest, there are a lot of people who are jealous or threatened by the success of others. It can be triggering to see another succeed in an area or space you want to thrive in. It might mean that if they're winning, you're losing. Don't believe this false narrative because it's so not true.

There is more than enough success, opportunity, and resources to go around. Period. That's why I make it my business to celebrate and applaud every win in our community. Our sisterhood is bigger than the things that divide us. If you see a mujer doing the things you want to do, learn from them. Ask them to mentor or coach you. Give them their flowers. Remember, today might be their turn but your time is coming. We should always be celebrating each other.

In case you haven't noticed there are a lot of us out here in these streets. And there is power in our collective strength and representation. We will not be denied. We will not go unnoticed. We will not stand by as others take credit for our work, get paid almost twice as much as we do, or get the promotions we have earned and worked hard for. When we lead with cultura, we are opening the door for other Latinas to show up, take up space, and unleash their awesomeness.

Not a lot of other people are going to do this for us. So really, the assignment is to do this for each other.

Embrace the next generation

"It wasn't like this when I was coming up in corporate." That's right. It wasn't. In some ways, showing up as a Latina at work these days feels easier and might be met with less resistance or judgement. While this might be true, there still aren't enough of us represented and it's still pretty hard to rise through the ranks in spaces that are predominantly white or male.

In spite of the challenges, younger generations are showing up fully and stepping into more critical and visible roles. They are experiencing success based on their own values and purpose. If you have been around longer, there could be the temptation to think these young women need to put in their time and respect the experience of those who came before them. My position is that we are here to learn from each other. There are lessons we can share with them and there are new and interesting perspectives the younger generation can share with us. Don't be too quick to dismiss people based on their age, role, or years of experience.

Instead, listen to what others have to say. Be curious about why they might see things differently. Create space for people that are different from you. Use the opportunity to grow together. Know that each of us brings something uniquely beautiful into the world. Be the kind of person who seeks out that beauty in others.

Be humble as you lead. Bringing others with you may require you to be vulnerable, to say you don't know, or to admit that you're scared. Being vulnerable in this way is not a sign of weakness. It is actually a strength to acknowledge fear or that you don't have all the answers. It's an invitation for others to rally around you and fill in the gaps. It's a way for Latinas of all nationalities, age groups, and educational backgrounds to work together for the community and beyond. A true leader will bring people together to lift all boats.

Pave the way

The best way you can show up as a good leader is by taking up space and using your voice. When you do this consistently, you are modeling to others the behaviors they should espouse on their journey toward leadership.

As I described at the beginning of this chapter, I was inspired by my manager. I saw her be brave and bold when situations called for it. She was firm, but fair. She spoke out when needed but mostly people came to her for advice or direction because she had developed a solid reputation as a knowledgeable leader. I was watching her lead. And so were many others. We saw her step into her power time and time again without fear or doubt. She was admired by senior leaders too. They saw her as a risk taker and someone who knew not only how to develop products but people too. She was on the fast track because she had done all the things and still had managed to bring others along. I looked up to her immensely.

These days, I strive to be more like my manager. I want to be the leader I've needed over the course of my career. You are lucky if you've had people in your life who have demonstrated interest in your development and advancement. Not everyone experiences this. In fact, as a Latina and Woman of Color, more often than not I find myself on the defensive in work situations, defending why I made a certain decision or took a specific action. Or why I'm deserving of an opportunity or special recognition. When I think about what I would have wanted or needed in a leader, it's things like appreciation for my contributions, confidence in my abilities, trust in my decisions, and a desire to really see me thrive and grow. I almost never had a manager that supported me in this way and so it is the way I choose to show up for others.

I mentor, coach, and support other Latinas and Women of Color as much as I can. I take intro calls all the time with people I meet online or at networking events. I offer advice, tips and connect individuals with people in my network who I think can help them move closer to their goals. I shine a light on mujeres that are doing incredible things and making an impact in their industries. I raise the visibility for women in my network regardless of their age, role, or background. I partner with others whose missions are aligned with my own. I am not afraid to give generously to the women in my community because it takes NOTHING away from me. This is something we should be doing constantly and consistently. Many of the Latina leaders I know operate this way too. It's great to see us show up for each other.

Trust that I will never forget where I'm from or how hard I've worked to get to where I am. And because of that, I will never forgo an opportunity to make the journey just a little easier for someone else.

En resumen

Embrace our shared cultura to strengthen the impact you make in the world. Stand together with other Latinas who share your mission and purpose. Together, we can create a bigger impact. Allow yourself to learn and grow by collaborating with others.

Stay open to learning, even as you lead. Leading doesn't mean you have all the answers and that your way of doing things is the only way. I find that when I partner with people that think differently, we end up with an even greater outcome. It's like the idea that 1 + 1 = 3. Our collective power and influence are greater than anything we try to do on our own. Be the type of leader who recognizes this and bring others along with you for greater impact.

Paving the way for others may look different for each of us. I like to create more space for other people. That is my way of leading. Being generous and sharing the spotlight with others.

You might decide to lead differently. Maybe you will focus on mentoring others, or hiring more underestimated talent on your team, or starting a nonprofit that serves underestimated young people. As the saying goes, "Para los gustos se hicieron los colores."[21] In other words, do you. What I want you to recognize is that giving of yourself freely and sharing yourself without any expectations is a great way to show up for other people. My manager never expected anything from me. And if I'm honest, that is what makes her way of being so great. There was no agreement or understanding that if she did something for me, I would have to do something for her in return.

My success was her success.

Her sponsorship was given to me freely. And what I took away from that experience was to pay it forward in the same way.

As we move into the next and final chapter, I want to share a few questions for reflection:

---

[21] This refrán loosely translates to "There's a color for every taste." It reminds me of the English phrase "To each their own." This saying reflects that everyone has different preferences and that's perfectly fine. Respecting the preferences and choices of others is the key message of this refrán.

1. How do you show up for our community?

   _____
   _____
   _____

2. How do you create space for others to learn and grow alongside you?

   _____
   _____
   _____

3. What are the qualities of leaders who made the biggest impact on you?

   _____
   _____
   _____
   _____

4. How have you learned from others in your leadership journey and what have those lessons taught you?

　_____

　_____

　_____

　_____

CHAPTER 12

AHORA, IT'S YOUR TURN

"Ya te puedes casar."[22]

---

[22]This refrán loosely translates to "Now you can get married." and is mostly used in a fun and loving way. Friends and family use this refrán to imply that you have acquired the experience or skill necessary for adult responsibilities (and therefore you are ready for something as significant as marriage). Playfully celebrating progress or readiness is the key message of this refrán.

"I say YES to opportunities that align with the impact I want to make." This quote appears on my website. It's critical for me to share with would-be clients and customers that I'm not just here looking to make money. I'm in this work to make an impact. I want to partner with others who are aligned with my values and purpose.

If you take nothing else away from reading this book, surely you can recognize that we all carry lessons passed down to us through refránes and sayings, key life figures, and lived experiences that shape who we are today. In this last chapter, I want you to reflect on your own journey and transformation. How has it unfolded so far and what have you discovered about yourself along the way? What lessons have you learned and what tips are you eager to share with others? Who has inspired you and in what ways? How will you use this inspiration for the greater good of the comunidad and the next generation?

There is magic in telling your story. In hearing others say, "Me too!" or "The same thing happened to me!" There are not enough Latinas sharing our experiences and points of view. There are not enough of us telling the younger generation, "We see you and we got you." There are not enough of us brave enough to call out the crap we've had to endure in corporate spaces that have kept us from reaching our fullest potential. Truly, we need more Latinas out here making noise, taking up space, and reclaiming what is ours. We need more of us here saying ENOUGH! ¡BASTA! with the racism, the misogyny, and the bias that keep us down, that seek to silence us, that desire to make us feel less than.

Telling our stories is a form of revolution. It's something each of us can do and must do for ourselves, for our families, and for our community. I know coming out of the shadows, as it were, is scary. And sometimes—actually most of the time—we will have to do it alone. Yet, we have the wisdom and the resilience of our ancestors to fuel us, to inspire us, to nourish us, and to hold us up in the most challenging of moments. When we learn to use our perceived "weaknesses" as our strengths, we change the narrative that has been fed to us for generations and we create realities that our parents and abuelos would be proud of.

So how does one go about telling their story? How does one begin to inventory their life experiences and dissect them in such a way that reveals valuable lessons they can both share with others and carry forward? How does one reclaim the power they always had but were told they didn't have or were afraid to use?

Instead of waiting until the end to share my reflection questions, I'm going to share them here:

- What defining moments or lessons from your journey have shaped who you are today?
- How have your unique experiences shaped the way you tackle challenges and seize opportunities?

- What legacy do you want to build for the next generation of Latinas in the workplace?
- What's stopping you from stepping into your power and leading the way?

Take the first step

It starts with saying YES.

Yes, to owning your narrative and stepping into your power. Yes, to not allowing others to dictate what the next step is for you and how long it will take you to get there. Yes, to owning your cultura and receiving what your family has passed down to you. Yes, to receiving gifts from our ancestors. Yes, to believing in yourself and trusting that you will make good decisions. Yes, to establishing boundaries that make sense for you and to having the courage to enforce those boundaries every time you need to. Yes, to believing that you know what's best for you. Yes, to living in your purpose and establishing lifelong values that will guide every decision you make about work, relationships, and life. Yes, to knowing that beyond your given family, there is a chosen family out there waiting for you and ready to love and accept you as you are.

Yes, to building communities wherever you find them and to being a positive contributing member of those communities. Yes, to lifting up others in the spirit of abundance because there is enough opportunity and success for everyone. Yes, to leading, learning, holding space, encouraging others, and otherwise holding up a mirror for your sisters when they need it the most to remind them that they are perfect as they are. Yes, to prioritizing your wellness, to not feeling guilty about eating right, moving your body, and loving every inch of who you are unapologetically. Yes, to making time to rest and being gentle with yourself. Yes, to taking up space and using your voice for things that matter. Yes, to being fearless as you advocate for yourself and others. Yes, to not shrinking or dimming your light. Yes, to pushing through the discomfort because on the other side of fear is the freedom you want and deserve. Yes, to giving yourself permission to go after the deepest desires of your heart. Yes, to showing up for yourself, to dreaming big, to asking others to help you, and to moving with intention as you advance toward your goals. Yes, to not settling and to asking for what you want. Yes, to clarity that allows you to move in the direction you want to go and to the risks that come with chasing what is in your heart. Yes, to showing up as your full self, to not compromising your values, and to walking with conviction.

Yes, to knowing who you are and recognizing that there is power in this knowing. Yes, to remaining steadfast and positiva. To dusting ourselves off and getting back in the game. Yes, to not gatekeeping but instead pouring love into others. Yes, to being happy for others as you wait for your time to come. Yes, to believing that your time will come. Yes, to counting your blessings and living a life filled with gratitude and appreciation for what you already have and for what is coming. Yes, to being patient and excited for what the Universe will bring. Yes, to dealing with setbacks like a fucking queen. Yes, to knowing that there is power in numbers. Yes, to showing up for other Latinas. Yes, to teaching and learning. Yes, to remaining curious and knowing that valuable lessons can come from any situation and anyone. Yes, to being a vulnerable leader who can admit they don't know everything. Yes, to being the leader you needed in your career and yes, to coaching and supporting others freely. Yes, to embracing our cultura to strengthen our impact. Yes, to sharing our unique gifts with others and not expecting a damn thing in return.

YES, YES, YES. One thousand times yes!

And keep saying YES because every yes is a step toward growth, alignment, and receiving what is meant for you.

Please note you may have to say yes more than once. Because sometimes life be life-ing and we start to second-guess our resolve. People will make us feel like maybe we don't have all the power we think we have. Or maybe we are not worthy of the life we want. Or maybe we don't deserve good things. Or indirectly, they tell us to "stay in our place."

Haters gonna hate. Shut that shit down. Remind yourself you are worthy and deserving. Confide in an amiga and listen as she reminds you of how amazing you are. Reflect on your journey and remind yourself why it's important for you to stick to your goals and be led by your purpose. Sometimes there will be people close to you that don't like the change.

Jefa, it will be on you to decide your next move.

My hope is that you will make decisions that lead you to the most fulfilling life you can have. That you will choose to put yourself first because doing that will lead to the greater good for so many.

I'll remind you now that saying YES may mean saying NO to beliefs that no longer serve you. I know when I hear anyone utter the words "Calladita te ves más bonita," that shit feels like someone is scratching their nails on a chalkboard. I categorically reject the belief that my silence should be used for the comfort and pleasure of others. Fuck that. I will speak when and if it's safe to do so, to the degree that I want, about whatever subject I deem necessary.

PERIOD.

A lot of what keeps me saying YES is being really clear on my WHY. So, I challenge you to work toward that clarity because it will make every future decision much easier. Does this align with my goals and personal vision, YES or NO? It's usually pretty clear. Occasionally, it's not and then I make the best decision with the information I have. Sometimes, I still make the wrong decision. But when I get that feeling that tells me there is a misalignment, I'm able to get myself back on track. Sometimes quickly. Sometimes, I have to be strategic and pace myself. But I know. And I trust myself. And because of that, I can move with intention until I get back to where I need to be.

Trust the process

Life will wait for no one. Sometimes we have to build the plane as we are mid-flight to our next destination. That's pretty much the case here. You may decide you are ready to live this new life, to write your own story, to step into your power. It's a process that can unfold quickly because you have already done a lot of the work required. Or it can take some time because you are playing catch-up. Wherever you find yourself in the continuum, do the work that's needed and keep going.

I wouldn't wait until you have all the answers to start living the life you want and desire. Start living that life today. Start making the shifts necessary that will lead you in the direction you want to go. Start noticing what you could do differently, then make the adjustments required. Start taking the time you need to decide whether something is aligned with your purpose. Start building the relationships that will sustain you during the difficult moments. Start asking for help, coming out of the shadows, owning your cultura, being unapologetic, and walking with conviction today.

There's no need to wait for a future time when everything is 100 percent defined and documented. You can start now and adjust as needed. Start now and just keep going knowing that mistakes will come, misalignment may arise, and boundaries will need to be set. I would argue that once you start, you will get hooked on all of the great outcomes you begin to experience and that will propel you to continue along your journey and live your truth.

Build community as you go. Find your people. Know that some people will appear as your people at first and then you may find out that they are in fact not your people. Not everyone is built like us. Some people are only looking to elevate themselves and will use you as a stepping stone for their good, not yours.

Sometimes it be your own people and your own friends.

Read that shit again. Cause it's true and I don't want you to get caught off guard when it happens. Not everyone will be for us. We already know this because we've seen it before. It's disappointing, and when we realize it, we just have to keep it moving. Take care of yourself. Shower yourself with self-love and self-acceptance. You know who you are and why you do the things you do. Ground yourself in that.

Love yourself, accept yourself, believe in yourself, and trust yourself. That's all power. A very high-power frequency. Step into that power with grace, humility, and courage. Allow everything else to fall to the side.

Bring others with you

I want you to know how much it means for you to not only do what is right for your own life and journey but to understand what a difference it makes to use your power to shine the light on others and bring them with you.

Many debate what constitutes a good leader. I say it's someone who owns their shit and who will use any influence they have to create space for other people. A true leader knows that they lead best when they recognize the contributions of others. When they remain curious and are open to learning and growing alongside others, regardless of role or educational background. Some people get caught up in the power and influence they obtain. A true leader sees power and influence as the ability to advocate for others. "Great, now I have a platform and people are listening. How will I use this for the greater good?"

Advocating for others is extremely important to me. Extremely. Probably because I want to be the person I always wished I had in my career. I worked for that one amazing manager for about three years. The balance of my thirty-year career was spent working for people that didn't always have my best interests in mind. That's why I want to be a force in the world that's showing up differently. And I want you to do the same. Be the representation you always wanted but never got. That can be a very powerful North Star.

En resumen

I started off this book by telling you that it's not a blueprint or template for you to follow. Mostly because I created my path based on my lived experience, the people I met along the way, and the values and purpose that drive me. Your path will be determined by the things that happen to you, the people you meet along the way, and what matters to you the most. Therefore, it stands that all of our stories will be different.

Still, some of my lessons might prove valuable to you, and if they do, please take them with you. Use what you can, what makes sense, what applies, and leave the rest. You will be building your own story based on your unique experiences and I look forward to where telling that story will take you.

This is an ongoing journey. I'm not done telling my story. It's still unfolding. I'm still learning. I'm still making mistakes and course correcting, as needed. I'm still making bad decisions. I'm still hitching myself to the wrong wagon. Shit happens. And we can't be too hard on ourselves when it does.

I am much more aware of my values and purpose than I've ever been. I am braver and bolder and more intentional than I was when I started. I am getting better at making decisions that will have positive outcomes. I am getting better at trusting myself and at showing up fully in every space I enter. I am more fearless in the face of adversity. I am more excited about the things that are coming and the community I'm building to support and encourage me along the way. I'm better at setting boundaries and sticking to them. I'm better at remaining positive even when I'm knocked down repeatedly.

Recommit yourself to this journey every day and I promise you too will reap the fruit of your labors. Saying yes is hard work. It's not easy and I won't pretend that doing so will result in a perfect life. What I can say is that you will be more content, more peaceful, and more confident. You will be fearless in ways you never imagined. Your heart will sing more, and your life will be bigger than your wildest dreams. You will attract more of what matters and you will live more fully.

Your voice matters. Being brave and bold matters. Owning your narrative matters. Bet on yourself, hermana. Yo voy a ti.[23]

---

[23] This Puerto Rican refrán loosely translates to "I believe in you." It reminds me of the English saying "I'm rooting for you." Friends and family use this refrán to express, in a heartfelt way, that they are ready to help or stand by you. Love and support are the key messages of this refrán.

ACKNOWLEDGEMENTS

I want to say thank you to so many people.

First, I want to thank those who were dismissive of me. You taught me the true value of kindness. To those who used me for their own gain, thank you for showing me the importance of trusted partnerships. And to those who doubted me, a special thanks. You taught me to be my own fiercest advocate. Because of you, I am stronger, bolder, and more unapologetically myself. You reminded me just how important it is to show up for me.

Next, I want to thank my family and friends for keeping a straight face when I said I was writing a book. I had long given up my dream of becoming an author. I wasn't sure I had the type of story the world needed to hear. And worse, I worried about the timing given the state of our nation. But your unwavering confidence in me, your love through the hard times, and your respect for my need to share this message with the world gave me the strength and courage to see it through.

I want to thank my book coach, Stacy, for her constant support, reassurance, and encouragement. You gifted our cohort with an easy way to transition into the writing process. Once the outline was completed, I felt so confident that I would get the words out. I appreciate your constant reminder that our stories matter and that we all have a story the world needs to hear.

I want to thank my editors, publisher, and illustrator for your partnership and expertise. When I started this project, I had no idea I'd be collaborating with such an incredible team of Latinas and other amazing women. What a gift to create something so meaningful together. I'm incredibly proud of the team that brought this book to life. THIS BOOK IS FOR ALL OF US.

To my content editor, Sandi, thank you for being the first person to read my manuscript! I appreciate you being so affirming as you provided me with feedback that would help to make the book better. Your kindness helped me trust the process and be open to all the great suggestions you made. You helped to take my manuscript to the next level, and if I had the chance, I would choose you again!

To my copy editor, Johanie, thank you for helping my baby shine! Your insights elevated my work, and your generosity gave me the confidence to own this manuscript. I'm beyond grateful for your support!

To my illustrator, Sol, thank you for turning my vision into something truly magical. Your creativity and eye for beauty made the cover a piece of art I'll never stop admiring. I'm so grateful you shared your talents with this project.

To the team at Publish Your Purpose, I am forever grateful for your role in helping me to get to the finish line and bring my book into the world. Your expertise and care showed every step of the way.

Acknowledgements

To the incredible community of Latinas who lift me up and support my work: my Lean In Latina sisters, the women of the Latina Writing Comunidad, and the many Latina authors in my network, thank you for showing up and showing out!

A special thank you to Anna Dapelo-Garcia, Founder & President of Lean In Latinas, for your beautiful foreword and for being an incredible partner in uplifting Latinas wherever we find them. Nothing says comunidad more than mujeres helping other mujeres rise.

Shout out to Giovanna "Gigi" Gonzalez, author of *Cultura and Cash*, who made the author journey look fun and easy and who did not gatekeep but instead shared her entire process and list of resources with anyone who was interested. Gigi, watching you pour so much of yourself into your book inspired me to write mine. Gracias for paving the way for all of us!

I want to thank all of the people who followed my writing journey, who read an early copy of the book and provided an endorsement or review, or who otherwise validated that this book was needed in the world. You showed up for me when it mattered most. Thank you.

I'd be remiss if I didn't give a special shoutout to Puerto Rican singer, rapper, and international superstar Benito Martínez Ocasio, aka, Bad Bunny. Your album *DeBÍ TiRAR MáS FOToS* (DTMF) kept me company throughout my writing journey and filled me with endless orgullo. I poured so much care into this book and a lot of it was fueled by the beautiful songs and powerful lyrics of DTMF. #YOSOYDEPFUCKINGR

Lastly, I want to thank Mami, Papá, and all of my abuelos, abuelas, and ancestors who helped shape me into the woman I am today. I am that woman because of the sacrifices you made, the dreams you dared to dream, and the hope you kept alive.

Quien tiene familia, tiene un tesoro.[24]

---

[24]This refrán loosely translates to "Whoever has family has a treasure." It's a reminder to count our blessings and appreciate the love and support of our given or chosen families. Gratitude and appreciation are the key messages of this refrán.

ABOUT THE AUTHOR

Hady Méndez is a NY-based best-selling author, Latina speaker, and ERG coach. She is the founder and CEO of Boldly Speaking LLC, a company that is transforming the professional experiences of underestimated professionals by providing them with the skills to rise and thrive in the corporate world or in whatever path they choose.

With a diverse career spanning over thirty years, Hady has served as head of equality for a major tech firm, held multiple customer-facing roles in high tech and financial services, served as a leader and advisor across various ERGs, dedicated two years to working with incarcerated and formerly incarcerated women internationally, and served as Community School Director at an elementary school in the South Bronx.

Hady's academic credentials include a Bachelor of Science degree in Computer Information Systems from Manhattan College, and graduate certificates in eBusiness and eCommerce from New York University and New Jersey Institute of Technology, respectively. She also holds a Family Development Credential from the University of Connecticut.

Hady is the Director of Programs for Lean In Latinas, an organization that is focused on advancing Latinas in the workplace, and the former Membership Lead for the NYC chapter of Ellevate Network, the largest community of women at work.

Hady's essays have been featured in *Business Insider* and #WeAllGrow Latina. Her thought leadership has been leveraged by organizations such as the Diversity Leadership Alliance, PowerToFly, Prospanica, and many others. Hady is a Latinas in Tech Luminarias 2022 honoree, a Women of ALPFA 2023 Latinas to Watch, a 2024 LinkedIn Top Coaching & Mentoring Voice, and the recipient of HACE's 2025 Mujer Maravilla Award.

In her free time, Hady is an amateur street art photographer and an avid podcast listener.

WANT MORE OF THIS ENERGY IN YOUR WORKPLACE?

Learn about Hady's programs, workshops, and coaching offerings or just say hi!

www.boldlyspeakingllc.com
www.linkedin.com/in/hadymendez
hadyunfiltered.substack.com
hola@calladitanomore.com

The B Corp Movement

Dear reader,

Thank you for reading this book and joining the Publish Your Purpose community! You are joining a special group of people who aim to make the world a better place.

What's Publish Your Purpose About?
Our mission is to elevate the voices often excluded from traditional publishing. We intentionally seek out authors and storytellers with diverse backgrounds, life experiences, and unique perspectives to publish books that will make an impact in the world.

Beyond our books, we are focused on tangible, action-based change. As a woman- and LGBTQ+-owned company, we are committed to reducing inequality, lowering levels of poverty, creating a healthier environment, building stronger communities, and creating high-quality jobs with dignity and purpose.

As a Certified B Corporation, we use business as a force for good. We join a community of mission-driven companies building a more equitable, inclusive, and sustainable global economy. B Corporations must meet high standards of transparency, social and environmental performance, and accountability as determined by the nonprofit B Lab. The certification process is rigorous and ongoing (with a recertification requirement every three years).

How Do We Do This?
We intentionally partner with socially and economically disadvantaged businesses that meet our sustainability goals. We embrace and encourage our authors and employee's differences in race, age, color, disability, ethnicity, family or marital status, gender identity or expression, language, national origin, physical and mental ability, political affiliation, religion, sexual orientation, socio-economic status, veteran status, and other characteristics that make them unique.

Community is at the heart of everything we do—from our writing and publishing programs to contributing to social enterprise nonprofits like reSET (https://www.resetco.org/) and our work in founding B Local Connecticut.

We are endlessly grateful to our authors, readers, and local community for being the driving force behind the equitable and sustainable world we are building together.

To connect with us online, or publish with us,
visit us at www.publishyourpurpose.com.

Elevating Your Voice,

Jenn T Grace

Jenn T. Grace
Founder, Publish Your Purpose

www.ingramcontent.com/pod-product-compliance
Lightning Source LLC
Chambersburg PA
CBHW060514090426
42735CB00011B/2223